PRAISE FOR *FULLY ENG*

"This book makes it really clear that the secret to education is enrollment. Not butts in seats, but human beings, eager to go on a journey."

—Seth Godin, author

"Perhaps more deeply than any other teachers I've encountered, Michael Matera and John Meehan understand that school needs a reboot, that students are the end users of a system that simply doesn't get them. The system misunderstands motivation, it ignores engagement, and it pays lip service to the fundamentals of what it takes to get students learning more deeply. Springing from amazing work in the classroom, this irresistible book will guide a new generation of teachers who desperately want something better for their students: schools that embrace them as the endlessly curious, restless, optimistic learners they are."

—Greg Toppo, author

"*Fully Engaged* is THE book that you need to read NOW. You're going to get ideas that are so simple and easy to implement they're ready for you to go go go. Matera and Meehan have done it. I hope you hop on the *Fully Engaged* train for a ride, because all of your students deserve it."

—Adam Welcome, author, podcaster, and educator

"This book had my brain buzzing with ideas to not only amp up student engagement, but also to help every individual feel confident and supported in the classroom. It was a refreshing reminder that both teaching and learning are meant to be fun and feel like play, and it provided concrete strategies to shift lesson plans into student-centered learning experiences. This was not one of those books that read like a how-to manual. Instead, John and Michael beautifully weave different scenarios for the reader to imagine. It was as if I were taking a peek into classrooms where these activities were playing out. I finished the book feeling energized and excited about teaching and full of actionable ideas to bring into my classroom."

—**Stacey Roshan,** educator and author

"I confess I am not the intended audience for this book: I don't like games, hate competition, and teach advanced, college-preparatory literature and film classes that often get deep into intellectual discussions that last over an hour. But guess what? I loved this book. John and Michael have compiled a guide bursting with ideas for all kinds of teachers, no matter what age or content they teach. I had a-ha moments in every chapter: new ways to introduce blackout poetry; suggestions for how to replace reading quizzes with high-energy curriculum quests; even ideas for how to make dreaded English annotations fun. I'm so excited thinking about where this book can help me take my students' learning. I'm getting copies for all my own kids' teachers!"

—**Alexis Wiggins,** author

"*Fully Engaged* is the perfect title for this book. From the beginning, I found myself taking notes and thinking about how all of these practical ideas could be infused into our classrooms. It provides not only the *why* but, just as importantly, the *how*. It's an outstanding read, and one I would recommend to anyone leading any group of people, young or old."

—**Joe Sanfelippo,** superintendent and author

FULLY ENGAGED

MICHAEL MATERA & JOHN MEEHAN

FULLY ENGAGED

PLAYFUL PEDAGOGY FOR REAL RESULTS

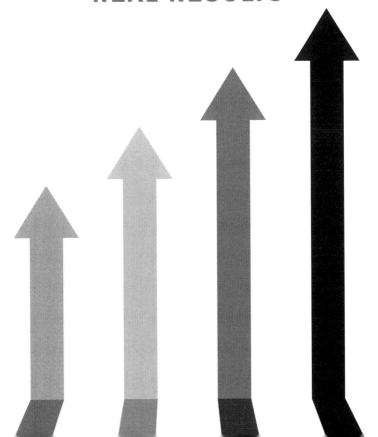

Fully Engaged: Playful Pedagogy for Real Results
© 2021 Michael Matera and John Meehan

This book is available at special discounts when purchased in quantity for use for educational purposes or as premiums, promotions, or fundraisers. For inquiries and details, contact the publisher at books@daveburgessconsulting.com.

Published by Dave Burgess Consulting, Inc.
San Diego, CA
DaveBurgessConsulting.com

Library of Congress Control Number: 2021941994
Paperback ISBN: 978-1-951600-94-5
Ebook ISBN: 978-1-951600-95-2

Cover design by Kapo Ng
Interior design by Liz Schreiter
Editing and production by Reading List Editorial: readinglisteditorial.com

To our families and the incredible community of Engagement Engineers at EMC² Learning. Thank you for your love and support, for believing in us, and for joining in this incredible journey to change the world.

This is for you.

CONTENTS

GAME OVER

What's past is prologue;
what to come, in yours
and my discharge.

—William Shakespeare, *The Tempest*

In ancient Greece, Socrates was regarded as the wisest teacher ever to have lived. It wasn't because he pretended to have all of the answers. Instead, he became the most famous philosopher in all the land because he knew how, when, and why to ask the right questions. And each time his clever students offered an answer, Socrates would plead his trademark ignorance. Rather than playing the know-it-all and simply telling his students whether they were right or wrong, Socrates would challenge the young learners in his charge to dig deeper, explain their thinking, and search for bold new solutions. Smiling knowingly, the wise old man might well have said something along the lines of: "Hmmm. Very interesting! And why do you think that?"

After all, it is Socrates who reminds us that "the unexamined life is not worth living."

Try as we might, we're not Socrates. So we probably shouldn't pretend to have all the answers, either. But it doesn't take a Greek philosopher to tell us that our modern-day education system is in serious need of some self-examination, no?

Because now, as countless educators struggle to keep pace with the increasingly personalized and fast-paced world outside of academia, it seems like so many of our schools that were built largely on antiquated systems of student compliance have started to crumble.

Yet it's an indisputable fact that Socrates never owned an iPad, so if we're looking to transform our schools into places where our students are fully engaged, we probably don't need all kinds of fancy computer software or expensive technology to get the job done. We need to start asking better questions! In classrooms around the globe, teachers hunger for strategies that can inspire authentic engagement, while young minds yearn for a new world of learning where they can become the hero. We crave choice. Mastery. And a clear sense of purpose.

But there is hope.

Legend speaks of a Timeless Temple of the Fully Engaged Classroom that has the power to restore our noble profession to an awe-inspiring era of wonder and joy. Before you lies an invitation to join us on the lesson-planning adventure of a lifetime. Our goal in writing this book is to help teachers unearth some of education's longest-held and most powerful secrets. We'll explore literally hundreds of ways that educators can combine the groundbreaking science of gamification with some of the most timeless cornerstones of our craft in order to captivate the minds of students of any age. Along the way, we'll explore the surprising research behind how our brains are hardwired for play, and take a closer look at concrete teaching strategies we've designed to help you put these playful methods to work in your instruction. We'll close our adventure with a journey inside the Timeless Temple of the Fully Engaged Classroom, where we can't wait to show you countless treasures that teachers everywhere can use to inject curiosity, wonder, joy, and excitement into any classroom. With a playful heart and an explorer's spirit, we're not just changing the game; we're changing the world! And in the pages that follow, we've laid out everything you'll need to create schools powered by endless stores of student-centered energy that have the potential to deliver lasting change for the better of the entire education system.

A SNEAK PREVIEW INTO THE TRANSFORMATIONAL POWER OF PLAYFUL PEDAGOGY

So just what, exactly, does a day look like inside the fully engaged classroom? We don't want to spoil all of the surprises just yet. But let's take a quick peek at the sort of adventure you might find yourself encountering in our journey ahead.

We'll start with a micro-sized case study using two games that are probably familiar to most every household on the planet.

Ever find yourself in a fight with your sister when she took your favorite game piece in Monopoly? Or gotten mad at your little brother because he picked "your guy" in a video game like *Mario Kart* before you had the chance? Regardless of what game you're playing, even the smallest of choices in the early stages of play can be enough to get gamers really fired up—even in cases where there's *zero functional difference* between selecting "piece one" or "piece two"! In a very real way, you're already hooked from the moment you sit down to play. And whether you're about to spend a few hours moving a tiny metal token or power-sliding a pixelated go-kart, you've already got a rooting interest as you take to the road before you. Having selected the "thing" that will represent you in this game, you're immediately armed with a clearer sense of what's at stake in this epic struggle of you against the world. Do you have the business acumen to build a real estate empire straight from bankruptcy all the way to the Boardwalk? Are you ready to take to the track and burn some serious rubber (and maybe a few real-life friendships) in your quest to become the fastest racer in all of Mushroom Kingdom?

As the old saying goes: "What mighty contests rise from trivial things."

Games can teach us so much! And by studying how the best games are put together (heck, even by learning a few hard lessons from games that are decidedly un-fun like a certain popular title where players "Do not pass Go, do not collect $200"), teachers can borrow endless techniques to help our classrooms feel more inviting, risk rich, and rewarding for everyone involved. And in the case of Monopoly and *Mario Kart*, getting players fully engaged from the moment they sit down to play starts with a simple bit of theming and an incredibly low-stakes choice.

Now let's imagine we applied those same game mechanics to our instructional design. Research is overwhelmingly clear that voice and choice play a vital role in helping students feel empowered by their learning. So let's take a look at our own classrooms and see if we can learn a thing or two from this familiar pair of games.

HERE'S WHAT A SAMPLE DAY IN A CLASSROOM MIGHT LOOK LIKE "BEFORE"

Divide your class into six groups of four. Task each group with conducting some chunk of a larger assignment and inform them that they will be creating a small deliverable work product that they should be prepared to submit and defend by the end of class. Allot thirty minutes for the activity, then spend the remainder of the class period doing your best to curb a bunch of off-task chatter from a lethargic room full of students who couldn't be bothered to care less about this forgettable affair.

Watch the clock tick by for an agonizing half hour, and pray for the time to expire as student groups turn in a parade of halfhearted submissions that are clearly the work of only one or two members in each group, at most.

Excited yet? It gets worse: You've got just enough time between classes to brace yourself for the next class section. There, you'll have the chance to repeat the exact same dead-end lesson plan all over again for a new group of students—most of whom have already seen a million texts, TikToks, and tweets from their peers to warn them that today's class is going to be a total drag.

HERE'S WHAT THE EXACT SAME LESSON LOOKS LIKE WHEN STUDENTS ARE FULLY ENGAGED

An epic superhero anthem blares from your iPhone as students make their way inside your classroom. Wearing a sweet pair of black aviator sunglasses, you greet them at the door with a smile: "Welcome to mission control!" You take a quick scan down the clipboard in your hand and nod to each student one by one, as if confirming their security clearance to allow them entry into the classroom and whatever top-secret assignment awaits them on the other side of your doorway. There's an undeniable buzz in the air and a sea of curious faces as these young learners take their seats. In bold, comic-book-inspired font on a slide displayed on the overhead projector, students see their instructions: "Assemble yourselves into teams of cutting-edge researchers for a top-secret government mission, and stand by for further details." And to cap it all off, the instructions just so happen to be placed right alongside a massive countdown clock, where the precious seconds tick, tick, tick away, signaling that the activity will soon begin.

As students divide themselves into teams, they notice you've already labelled the six four-desk groups in your classroom as sectors "Alpha," "Bravo," "Charlie," "Delta," "Echo," and "Foxtrot." Once seated with their groups, students see a printed worksheet with the descriptions of four unique "mission" roles that will need to be filled within their team: commander, mechanic, engineer, or radio control—each of which comes preloaded with a special ability and uniquely assigned task of its own.

Once students have settled into their groups, you welcome this new class of recruits, and announce that there will be an epic Six-Sector Showdown once the top-secret mission countdown clock reaches zero. Set that big old countdown timer on the overhead and watch everyone race to work with a clearer sense of ownership and purpose for whatever pulse-pounding challenge lies on the other side of that countdown.

You can feel it, right?

That's where we're headed.

ED-VENTURE AWAITS

There's a lot to unpack in that sample fully engaged classroom, right? Themes, teams, timers, choice, competition, collaboration, stress, strategies, and . . . sunglasses? We haven't even rung the bell yet to signal the actual start of class! It's a lot to process all at once. To the ambitious, it sounds like a ton of work. To the skeptics, it might only seem like a whole lot of sugary fluff.

But don't worry: this guidebook will be with you at every step of the way.

It is often said that even the greatest journey begins with a single step. With that in mind, we've divided this book into stepwise chapters to help you make your way through the lesson-planning adventure of a lifetime. In our first two chapters, we'll dig deep into what gamification offers your classroom and take a look at some of the lingering problems that have resulted from entire generations getting caught up inside the "Game of School." We will discuss that game (and its pitfalls) in the first chapter. Then we'll walk you through the basics of a sweet science known as "classroom gamification," and take a deep dive into the serious studies behind why and how all this game stuff actually works in the first place. Real talk: we find massive tomes of educational theory to be just as dry as the next guy. So while these early pages are rooted in a good bit of background research on our end, fear not. We will keep things bite-sized and breezy so you'll never feel like you're drowning in data. Likewise, if you've already read either of our previous books, don't worry: We're not here to repeat ourselves! The chapters ahead provide all-new content to help you make your way to the next level of playful pedagogy. And from there, our Journey to the Timeless Temple of the Fully Engaged Classroom begins.

In chapters 3–6, we'll take a closer look at practical pedagogical shifts that we can make in our classrooms through concrete examples of game-inspired teaching strategies we're calling the "Pillars of Playful Learning." Think of it as your gamification guidebook, if you will. This is where we offer an action-packed how-to guide of lesson-planning ideas, plug-and-play resources, and high-energy classroom activities that can easily be adapted for any course or content area. And in it, we will explore:

Pillar I: Choice and challenge
Pillar II: Imagination and iteration
Pillar III: Teamwork and tasks
Pillar IV: Feedback and failure

Finally, we'll close our time together in a chapter we've devoted to "people and purpose"—a powerful testament to what we believe is, was, and always must remain at the center of this pedagogical quest. Also, to help us keep track of all the treasures we encounter as we go, we've included a series of reflection questions at the end of each chapter. We include these questions as a method to help you connect to and customize your adventure at each step along the way.

But we simply couldn't do an epic quest-inspired book's introduction any justice if we didn't take a quick opportunity to throw in a journey with more than one possible outcome. After all, every great journey begins with the hero hearing the call to adventure! But for their quest to begin, the hero must heed that call. And that volition is the first step toward creating a powerful change. As we'll soon discover, every great game depends on the choices its players will make. So let's open this adventure by making a choice of our own.

We call the other way the "Page-Nine Ending." It's probably familiar to a lot of teachers.

THE PAGE-NINE ENDING

It's another Monday morning and you trudge back into school carrying an overstuffed reusable grocery bag full of graded work. Not going to lie: the grades ain't pretty. The students have been checked out for weeks, and the day's lesson plan was shaping up to be a dud as it is, but you were simply up so late grading all of those papers—one halfhearted assignment after another—that you're fried before you even set foot in the classroom. You grab your trusty travel mug, grateful at least for a much-needed dose of caffeine to get through the morning, but plot twist! Your coffee is already lukewarm.

It's going to be a long day.

Bleary eyed with a cold cup of joe in your hands, you've got just enough time to head to your teacher mailbox before the first bell rings, and that's when you run into Geoff.

"Ugh. Mondays. Am I right?" he says with a frown.

You shake your head knowingly, and he proceeds to tell you how he's giving a big test today, and his students are simply refusing to sit still and behave. You know the feeling.

Rinse and repeat.

Another Monday in the Game of School.

Congratulations! Your quest is at an end.

So, will you read on? Or settle for the Page-Nine Ending?

If your educator journey seeks a fate beyond the comfort of the Page-Nine Ending, we are thrilled to begin this journey with you. Feel free to hit us up on Twitter @MrMatera or @MeehanEDU—use the hashtag #EMC2Learning—and we'll be happy to offer whatever information we can to help along the way. We promise we'll do more than reply with a quick "Hmmm. Very interesting! And why do you think that?"

Like we said, we're not Socrates, right?

Thank you so much for joining us on this epic adventure. We'll see you on the other side!

CHAPTER ONE

THE LOST FOUNDATIONS OF PLAY

*If you surrendered to the air,
you could ride it.*

—Toni Morrison, *Song of Solomon*

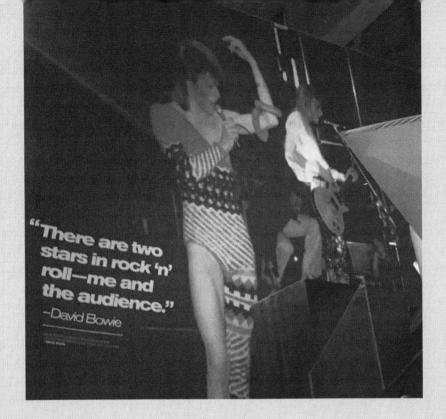

"There are two stars in rock 'n' roll—me and the audience."
—David Bowie

Hi, folks. John here! In October of 2017, I was wrapping up my tenure with the Bill & Melinda Gates Foundation's Teacher Advisory Council, and I had the chance to visit the Museum of Pop Culture (MoPOP) in Seattle, Washington. As soon as I walked into the MoPOP foyer, I was blown away by a massive, forty-foot-tall piece of wall art that led visitors up two flights of stairs toward the museum's David Bowie exhibit. There, in all his glammed-out Ziggy Stardust glory, was a towering image of this Rock and Roll Hall of Fame icon, his vibrant colors and wild hair on full display.

As a child who grew up on a steady diet of Bowie and the Rolling Stones, I was struck at the unexpected sight of this larger-than-life image of one of my dad's all-time favorite performers. But it was actually the quote positioned directly beside this giant portrait that sent my teacher brain reeling with possibilities:

"There are two stars in rock 'n' roll—me and the audience."

Unlike so many flash-in-the-pan performers that came before him and flamed out just as quickly, David Bowie was a bona fide rock star with staying power.

Year after year, Bowie seemed to have a finger on the pulse as if to remind the world that if he was going to be the Starman, he certainly couldn't do it alone. He constantly had to grow. To rebel. To anticipate. To empathize. And to "turn and face the strange." Over the course of a legendary career that spanned more than forty years, a once-quiet child from a quaint Brixton neighborhood made his fans feel like they were a fundamental part of the global phenomenon that he became.

Eminently colorful and always in motion, David Bowie was a living LEGO set.

A human Etch A Sketch.

In every sense of the word: a game-changer.

In fact, David Bowie has a whole lot in common with elements you'd find in the best games. Check out this description of the key elements of top-notch game design from Miguel Sicart, associate professor at the Center for Computer Games Research at IT University of Copenhagen, and tell us you're not picking up some serious David Bowie vibes: "Designing for play means creating a setting rather than a system, a stage rather than a world, a model rather than a puzzle. Whatever is created has to be open, flexible, and malleable to allow players to appropriate, express, act and interact, make and become part of the form itself."[1]

Classic Starman, right? His agency became his art.

What a contrast to the tired toxicity that plagues the Game of School—and what a powerful metaphor for the fully engaged classroom so many educators aspire to create.

---

1   Miguel Sicart, *Play Matters* (Cambridge, MA: MIT Press, 2014).

WHY WE NEED TO START BY SAYING "GAME OVER"

Most of us have probably heard about a phrase called the "Game of School." In a 2015 TEDx talk, Lincoln, Nebraska-based assessment and evaluation specialist Rob McEntarffer outlined the situation brilliantly:

> We play "The Game of School" when we enter a learning situation and we become more concerned with accumulating points and getting a grade and winning rather than any of the learning that's going on in that classroom. Some of the language we use about school reveals some of the elements of this game: What did you get on that test? What did she give you on that project? How many points did she dock you for it being late? Can I get extra credit for bringing Kleenex into this class?
>
> We know "The Game of School" isn't real learning. "The Game of School" isn't like a video game. Teachers don't zap learning into students. Learning isn't something that happens as a nice side effect when we go for the points and try to get an A. Real learning is transformative. Real learning changes something important about us.[2]

McEntarffer's point is spot on. Traditional schools have spent a lifetime conditioning students to focus only on the grade they've received. And when we focus only on the grade, the learning invariably suffers. Like some weird and slightly less dystopian take on *The Hunger Games*, we've created a toxic system where students compete in a sort of war of each against all for titles like "valedictorian," where only a select few each year can be declared the winner.

Here's a typical example of two fictional teachers and their students who are unwittingly caught up inside the Game of School in a classroom near you:

---

2 Rob McEntarffer, "The Game of School," filmed October 2015 at TEDxLincoln, Lincoln, NE, video, 12:07, tedxlincoln.com/speakers/2015/rob-mcentarffer.html.

Ms. Jones assigns nightly homework, but always errs on the side of compassion. She goes easy on her students with no more than fifteen minutes of assigned work per evening. "Remember, I'm grading you on completion, not on the number of problems you get correct," she tells her classes. But it doesn't take long before students realize that they can rack up an easy stack of freebie grades ("10 points for completed homework per night!") and roll into their next exam with a cool 100 or so points to their name, even if they might not have always put forth their most honest effort to complete these quick nightly assignments.

Students in Mr. Smith's class, however, are graded on how correct their homework is. Ten points per night! "After all," he tells you with a frown in the faculty lounge, "if I don't grade them on this work, then they certainly won't do it, will they?" Mr. Smith is a no-nonsense kind of guy who doesn't care much for the National PTA's famed "ten minute rule" which recommends that students should be assigned a daily maximum of no more than ten minutes of homework per grade level per night (so, for example, a fifth grader should have a total of fifty minutes of homework, distributed evenly across all of their subjects). And so, he routinely gives his students assignments that can easily take up to an hour's worth of time to complete. "Because these kids need to learn!" Feared for his notorious eye for accuracy, Mr. Smith is pleased to report that every one of his students dutifully completes their ten straight days of homework before the big test. With perfect answers across the board!

Except.

Deep down, we know all too well that at least a handful of students in Ms. Jones' class are getting their grades inflated as a result of simple homework completion. Ten out of ten every night for ten days in a row before the big exam gives them 100 easy points. But that's compliance, not comprehension. So even if they fail the unit test with a 60 percent, we just average it against their existing 100 points and call the grade an 80 percent for the unit. "Some kids are just bad test takers, I suppose," we shrug. Better luck next time. And just like that, we're on to the new unit.

Meanwhile, students in Mr. Smith's class are so terrified to get a single answer wrong that they usually send a text message or two each night to make sure they'll come back to school with the right answers filled out. Before you know it, students have set up a group chat where they're snapping photos of completed work, and the majority of scholars have suddenly found themselves inside of some nefarious quid pro quo homework syndicate ("you do history class; I'll do science") where everyone walks away with the right answers. One hundred points in the bank apiece before the dreaded test day, and whaddayaknow? That failing grade of a 60 percent can just be shrugged off as "a hard test"— easily averaged out when balanced with their other ill-gotten scores.

"Bs get degrees," right?

This happens time and again in countless classrooms across the country. Students earn points. They move up in levels. And if they're really lucky, perhaps they even rack up a handful of honor society plaudits to help pad their college resume by getting top grades in subject areas that they have no intention of studying after high school. But here's the dirty secret: there's a really good chance that our students have simply learned how to game the system itself. Second verse? Same as the first. No love. No reinvention. And certainly no stardust.

This Game of School is no more than a house of cards.

In short, *everyone* is getting played.

Not surprisingly, many students find themselves in never-ending states of high alert for fear of falling behind or getting exposed for their part in this elaborate charade. Research shows that stress levels of the average twenty-first century student are through the roof, with a 2014 study from the American Psychological Association confirming that: "Many teens also reported feeling overwhelmed (31 percent) and depressed or sad (30 percent) as a result of stress. More than one-third of teens reported feeling tired (36 percent) and nearly one-quarter of teens (23 percent) reported skipping a meal due to stress."[3]

Many students have become so numb to this constant state of stress that they feel like pawns who merely go through the motions and are all just a "part of the game." And since this game is so poorly designed, it doesn't take long before players start looking for whatever shortcuts they can find in order to claim the almighty high score. Cram. Cheat. Rinse. Repeat.

Enough is enough.

This is why we're starting our journey by saying "game over." Goodbye to an education system powered by widespread student cheating and record-level rates of teacher burnout. So long to a grade-obsessed academic thresher fueled by stacks of ungraded papers while millions of children get chewed up in never-ending anxiety spirals. And see you later to a soul-deadening parade of multiple choice exams that strips young minds of their intrinsic love of learning by reducing creative thought to binary machine logic. The myriad obstacles before us make it crystal clear that the old system simply is not working. We need to admit that if the traditional approach to school is in fact a game, it is a poorly designed one that routinely falls short of meeting the needs of so many of today's students.

The mark of any system's success is the least healthy behavior that it is willing to tolerate.

We need to hit the reset button.

A HARD RESET

So what is a game, anyway?

In his seminal 1978 work *The Grasshopper: Games, Life and Utopia*, Bernard Suits, a philosophy professor at the University of Waterloo in

---

3 Sophie Bethune, "Teen Stress Rivals That of Adults," *Monitor on Psychology* 45, no. 4 (April 2014): 20, apa.org/monitor/2014/04/teen-stress.

Ontario, argued that "playing a game is a voluntary attempt to overcome unnecessary obstacles."

In golf, we intentionally make it harder to put a tiny ball into a far-off hole simply by putting a few hundred yards between the two. In Scrabble, we're forced to dream up words using random combinations of only seven letter tiles at a time. And in *Super Mario*? Colorful graphics blink as we mash a precise combination of buttons at the exact right time, lest we fall into a pit and find ourselves left with no choice but to try, try again.

Truth be told, each of these games is a heck of a lot of work. And each game gets exponentially harder as we progress. But those epic moments when we're able to overcome these obstacles in our path? Well, that's where the joy comes from. That's what makes it a game.

A voluntary effort to overcome unnecessary obstacles.

In our own classrooms, these obstacles usually come in the form of sleepy, complacent, and compliant teaching practices. Fair warning: if we're setting out to change the education game, there's a good chance we will run into some pretty standard "sand traps" along the way—like antiquated teaching practices.

But we can escape these traps, thanks to our brush with the Starman.

His insight reminds us that there are always two stars in our classroom, and that the most enduring ch-ch-changes are only possible when we "turn and face the strange" and "let all the children boogie." It's not enough for our student audience to watch us take the stage. Nor is it even enough for teachers to merely transition to the role of "guide on the side." We need to do whatever it takes to connect with those we serve. To let them become the brilliant, beautiful forces of nature that each of them was born to be.

This starts by understanding the foundations of play.

STARTING FROM THE BOTTOM

Have you ever heard the heartwarming story of the Christmas Truce? Let's set the scene.

It was December of 1914 and the world was at war. In the muddy, blood-soaked trenches of Flanders, soldiers from the noble British army lobbed countless rounds of mortar shells and machine gun fire at the opposing Germans, who likewise hunkered down in makeshift holes of their own, surrounded by barbed wire and mustard gas. As the war raged on, thousands died on both sides of the battle from their daily armed conflicts. Thousands more died from cholera and other diseases brought on by the rat-infested battlefields and perpetual rain. It was, as the papers called it, the "Great War," and the bitterness between the two sides was deep-seated, violent, and unceasing.

Until Christmas, that is.

As the Smithsonian Institute explains:

> The first signs that something strange was happening occurred on Christmas Eve. At 8:30 p.m. an officer of the Royal Irish Rifles reported to headquarters: "Germans have illuminated their trenches, are singing songs and wishing us a Happy Xmas. Compliments are being exchanged but am nevertheless taking all military precautions." Further along the line, the two sides serenaded each other with carols—the German "Silent Night" being met with a British chorus of "The First Noel"—and scouts met, cautiously, in no man's land, the shell-blasted waste between the trenches. The war diary of the Scots Guards records that a certain Private Murker "met a German Patrol and was given a glass of whisky and some cigars, and a message was sent back saying that if we didn't fire at them, they would not fire at us."[4]

By the next afternoon, the opposing armies had reached an impromptu one-day ceasefire. Soldiers from both sides joined on the same fields where they'd previously been engaged in a bloody conflict to trade small gifts, sing songs together, and tell stories of their loved ones back home.

They even played soccer.

Hold up a minute. This was mere hours removed from some of the most brutal armed conflicts that the world had ever seen. So how on earth did these two sworn enemies come to a sudden mutual understanding where they agreed—even if only for a short while—to co-create a moment that stands forever as a testament to the very best of our shared humanity?

As the ageless saying reminds us: this is a classic case of Maslow before Bloom.

---

4   Mike Dash, "The Story of the WWI Christmas Truce," Smithsonianmag.com, December 23, 2011, smithsonianmag.com/history/the-story-of-the-wwi-christmas-truce-11972213/.

Self-actualization
desire to become the most that one can be

Esteem
respect, self-esteem, status, recognition, strength, freedom

Love and belonging
friendship, intimacy, family, sense of connection

Safety needs
personal security, employment, resources, health, property

Physiological needs
air, water, food, shelter, sleep, clothing, reproduction

"LEVELING UP" THROUGH MASLOW'S HIERARCHY

Perhaps you've heard the saying "Maslow Before Bloom," yes? In a 1943 paper titled "A Theory of Human Motivation," noted researcher Abraham Maslow presented a motivational theory of psychology as a five-tier model of human needs, often depicted as hierarchical levels within a pyramid. In Maslow's view, needs lower down in the hierarchy (basic physiological needs like air, water, and food—practical matters of safety like health and freedom from physical danger) must be satisfied before individuals can attend to needs higher up on the pyramid, like esteem and self-actualization. In "game" speak, it might help to think of these five tiers like they were different "levels" of play: the only way to "level up" to a subsequent challenge is to fulfill all requirements of the previous level.

The Christmas Truce is a testament to a playful spirit emerging from the trenches of even the most awful of circumstances one might imagine—almost like reaching a sort of elusive "bonus level." So let's see how these two opposing armies got there:

> **Levels One and Two:** Safety first! Scouts from the opposing armies served as "team captains" to ensure mutual safety as they hammered out the terms of a temporary ceasefire: You don't shoot us, we won't shoot you (physiological and safety needs).

Level Three: In recognition of the holiday, the "players" from both camps took turns singing beloved songs of their national origin, thereby humanizing each team to their opponents (love and belonging).

Level Four: In a mutual show of respect, unarmed soldiers from the opposing camps freely left their trenches, meeting their opponents in a neutral territory to exchange stories and small gifts (esteem).

Level Five: In a beautiful display of the shared humanity from all parties involved, the real-life enemies became friendly rivals and transformed what was once a battlefield into a temporary field of play (self-actualization).

If the Christmas Truce teaches us anything, it's that once an individual feels safe inside a shared world of play, there is simply no telling what amazing things they can accomplish. If a playful environment can bring a temporary stop to a war, there is no reason to believe that it couldn't work wonders in our classrooms. After all, we're not asking soldiers to risk their lives by trading bayonets for soccer balls. We're simply trying to convince the learners in our classroom to move beyond their comfort zones and gradually surrender to a playful spirit that will help them tackle their next quiz, test, or homework assignment.

This is "gamification."

Simply stated, gamification is about tapping into positive psychology by bringing in game-like elements and design techniques to things that aren't games. And once you know how to spot it, it's everywhere you look:

It's feeling a jolt of pride when you're invited to a "Members Only" sale at your favorite store or on the receiving end of an upgraded "Diamond Level" check-in status at your favorite airline.

It's that sense of satisfaction that comes from earning points toward a free beverage at your neighborhood coffee shop.

It's that rush of pleasant surprise that comes from getting pop-up notifications that your weekly screen time is down 12 percent from the previous seven days.

It's those tiny boosts of positive reinforcement each time you unlock streaks and badges in apps that track everything from personal fitness milestones to number of books read.

Gamification is used to recruit and retain customers, attract new clients, and create powerful bonds with teammates the world over. You'll find it hard at work in hospitals, health care agencies, the United States military, decorated institutions of higher learning, and in the corporate strategies of more than 70 percent of Fortune 500 companies including Disney, Google, Samsung, eBay, LEGO, American Express, Home Depot, and Amazon.[5]

Writing in an August 2020 article from UK-based *Training Zone* magazine, Terry Pearce, author and founder of the training company Untold Play, brilliantly observes that "gamification has unjustly garnered a bad name in the past but, when used properly, it's a perfect way of driving the behaviors you want to see in your learners. The key is to tap into the emotional, human core of the learning experience."

This doesn't just mean spending an odd day at the end of a unit playing class Jeopardy! or Kahoot! As Pearce explains, "Real gamification goes deeper. It's about exploring what motivates people to play games, and to keep playing." And here's the key part: "*It's about adapting those hooks and ideas, sometimes very subtly, always very carefully, to motivate people towards the behavior we want from them, in learning or anywhere else.*"[6]

Let's push this definition even further, because "gamification" doesn't mean simply "scoring points" or playing games in school. Merely adding points or slapping a paper-thin theme on an existing activity doesn't make it gamified, it makes it gimmicky. True

5 Alex Konrad, "Inside the Gamification Gold Rush," *Fortune*, October 17, 2011, fortune.com/2011/10/17/inside-the-gamification-gold-rush-2/.

6 Terry Pearce, "Gamification beyond the Buzzword: Why It's Not What You Think," *TrainingZone*, August 2, 2020, trainingzone.co.uk/deliver/training/gamification-beyond-the-buzzword-why-its-not-what-you-think.

gamification is about fostering autonomy, rewarding player curiosity, and responding to the meaningful choices that individuals make. It's about understanding positive psychology, user-centered design, and the awesome power of a flow state. And it's about creating a learning experience that's completely powered by intrinsic motivation.

In short: it's playing, with purpose.

And the story of the Christmas Truce is a powerful example of what incredible heights can be reached when individuals in even the most harrowing of circumstances feel free to surrender to a spirit of play. This perfect storm-of prerequisites leads us toward the series of gamification essentials that, from here on out, we'll refer to as our Timeless Temple of the Fully Engaged Classroom, supported evenly by four massive "Pillars of Playful Learning." The chapters ahead will offer hundreds of teaching strategies and practical resources inspired by each of those pillars in closer detail. But the entire structure is built on the following foundation:

FOUNDATION OF THE FULLY ENGAGED CLASSROOM:
All games depend on the free consent of all parties involved.

Whether we're talking about students, Starmen, or soldiers, it is crucial to note that none of these individuals were forced into the game against their will. As French philosopher Roger Caillois notes in 1958's *Man, Play and Games*:

> There is also no doubt that play must be defined as a free and voluntary activity, a source of joy and amusement. A game which one would be forced to play would at once cease being play. It would become constraint, drudgery from which one would strive to be freed. . . . Finally and above all, it is necessary that they be free to leave whenever they please, by saying "I am not playing anymore."[7]

The three magic words of any game: Consent. Consent. Consent. If players are not free to walk away at any time, then it's not a game. A fully engaged classroom must be safe and supportive, playful and purposeful, equitable and engaging for all students. And the first step in creating game-changing classrooms should always be ensuring the physical, emotional, and psychological safety of all parties involved. For far too long, the Game of School has been a joyless slog through the trenches, where there's only one way to play.

NOT ALL FUN AND GAMES

On the quest to change the game in education, it's imperative to begin with one important note: the goal should never be simply to replace an old system with a new one that is more "fun."

When employed correctly, gamification and game-based learning can be every bit as viable an instructional approach as a Socratic seminar, a flipped classroom, or a good old-fashioned group presentation. But as we have all learned, not every educational technique is appropriate for every audience and no single instructional strategy will work for every lesson plan, nor should it be forced to.

---

7 Roger Caillois, *Man, Play and Games*, trans. Meyer Barash (Champaign, IL: University of Illinois Press, 2001).

You wouldn't try to teach a room full of kindergarteners their ABCs by standing at the board and lecturing at them for forty-five minutes. You wouldn't teach Shakespeare's *Hamlet* to a high school class by asking them to go home and read the whole five-act play over the weekend before returning to school on Monday morning for a one-hundred-question ScanTron exam (at least we hope you wouldn't). And there are some instances where teachers simply have no business using game-based learning or gamified instructional strategies—particularly in cases where a student's mental wellbeing, an entire people's real-life trauma, and specific lessons involving certain historical topics are nothing to play around with.

Sorry to start this part of the chapter off on such a down note, gang. But we just can't stress this point enough when even a cursory search through materials currently available on Teachers Pay Teachers literally turns up *hundreds* of hits where educators are still creating all manner of Holocaust simulations and Underground Railroad escape rooms. The severity of the matter warrants a thorough disclaimer that bears repeating.

Seriously. Don't do this.

When we design classroom activities, we need to be especially mindful of the messages we send even without meaning to. We're sure you've seen a number of noteworthy horror stories of "simulation"-based lesson plans that have made headlines over the years and have caused harm, both to the students in the classroom and to the careers of the educators who attempted these activities, regardless of how well-intentioned they may have been. Every time we ask our students to "play pretend," it's vital to keep in mind the deeper messages these scenarios might inadvertently convey. Sometimes, even simulated stress can be a very real trigger. Remember that some simulations simply aren't school appropriate. As the Anti-Defamation League has observed:

> While simulation-type activities may appear to be a compelling
> way to engage students, [certain historical events] involving

genocide and oppression such as the Holocaust, slavery, racial segregation, Internment of Japanese-Americans, etc. . . . can be emotionally upsetting or damaging for students who are sensitive and/or who may identify with the victims.[8]

In these rare instances where you're dealing with lesson plans that bear close resemblance to traumatic real-life topics, please tread lightly or don't tread at all. We need to remain keenly aware that our lesson plans should always help learners make *sense* of what they're learning. Never to make *light* of actual trauma.

ALL STRESS IS NOT CREATED EQUAL

Here's the good news: While this stuff is incredibly serious, there is plenty of research to suggest that not all stress is created equal. Nor, in fact, is all stress even bad. That's why researchers often distinguish between *distress* (from the Greek word literally meaning "bad stress"), and its lesser-known cousin, *eustress* (also from the Greek, literally meaning "good stress," and powered by the same prefix as *euphoria*—a flood of positive feelings). With apologies to George Orwell: distress bad; eustress good. We feel eustress all the time, and often in some of our happiest moments. Particularly when we play games. It is the rush of endorphins that comes from a friendly soccer match. That last-second comeback that pulls off the upset victory. Or that feeling of landing on the sole remaining unclaimed property and being able to complete that missing piece to your colorful monopoly. Eustress comes from that momentary chance to lose yourself in the excitement that comes from chasing victory, lest you experience the devastating agony of defeat.

You're playing because you want to. And the eustress actually gets you excited to play the game. It's all the buzz of your fight-or-flight instincts without the pain of actual trauma, and research suggests

---

8 Anti-Defamation League, "Why Simulation Activities Should Not Be Used," adl.org/education/resources/tools-and-strategies/why-simulation-activities-should-not-be-used.

that eustress can be a powerful way to forge strong and lasting human connections. Take, for example, the work of Chris Gibbons from the School of Psychology at Queen's University Belfast, who's published over a dozen academic white papers on the subject. Here he is talking about how both types of stress play a major role as students adjust to university life (we've highlighted the best of the best):

> Social opportunities . . . were important to help new students integrate into [academic] life and to help them network and build support. Educators need to consider how course experiences contribute, not just to potential distress but to potential eustress. . . . Significant positive correlations were expected between the student experiences rated as potential eustress (uplifting ratings) and course satisfaction, motivation and feeling part of a learning community.
>
> It is likely that an effective way to [support students] is to promote initiatives for students to interact and network more with each other and not just during induction week but throughout the first semester.[9]

From the battlefields to the classrooms, the evidence is clear: "bad stress" makes us feel like we are in a fight for our lives. But "good stress" can actually help individuals feel connected and engaged. Gamification is really just eustress with a rulebook, and as we'll soon see, the rules for a gamified classroom activity don't even have to be all that fancy. The unspoken agreement in a gamified environment is that we're all friends here, and since we're playing on the same team, you're safe to take risks. We're talking serious "love and belonging"-level Maslow vibes right from the get-go, folks. Which means there's nowhere to go but up to those highest levels of the pyramid where players will naturally find themselves reaching for even higher purpose like "esteem" and "self-actualization."

---

9   Chris Gibbons, "Stress, Eustress and the National Student Survey," *Psychology Teaching Review* 21, no. 2 (Autumn 2015): 86–92, files.eric.ed.gov/fulltext/EJ1146635.pdf.

In other words, a student who is fully engaged will be *that much further* from feeling stuck in the trenches. *And that much closer* to achieving what otherwise might have seemed impossible.

Classroom gamification takes those same principles of what makes a great game—i.e., rules, obstacles, and a friendly spirit of competition—and applies them to an educational setting. It works because students are constantly reminded that they're safe and supported in a place where the teacher is serious about learning, yet they never take themselves too seriously. Students simply learn better when they feel connected to one another and the work that they do.

And the best part? Gamification doesn't have to mean year-long adventures, gimmicky rulebooks, or elaborately themed storylines. It can simply come from dialing up the eustress through incorporating more game-like elements in your instructional design. Let's take a look at some zero-prep-required examples of eustress in action to give a sense of the joy that lies along this road to that elusive Timeless Temple of the Fully Engaged Classroom.

PLAYING WITH EMPATHY STARTS YOUR CLASS OFF STRONG

Two Word Check In

A Fully Engaged Upgrade to getting a sense of your students' emotional temperature

Brené Brown might well be the world's leading expert on empathy. She's written a half-dozen books on the subject, and her TED Talk titled "The Power of Vulnerability" has been viewed close to fifty million times. Brown says that one of the best ways she knows to help remind the people she serves that they're all playing for the same team is to start each day with a quick, two-word check-in. She first shared this strategy during the COVID-19 pandemic. As an April 2020 article in *Inc.* magazine explains:

> The brilliance of this is two-fold: First, it's super short. It doesn't take long for everyone to give their answer. It gives permission for people to quickly name their feelings without judgement. Second, it acknowledges that we humans often feel many things at once.[10]

What an inclusive upgrade to traditional closed-ended attendance taking! What a validating way to take the emotional temperature of the room without making students feel like they need to be "good" every day of your instructional year. This helps us begin every class with the reminder that myriad emotions are welcome beyond the usual roll-call routine. Just a quick check-in with two words apiece—a simple "game" with exactly one rule.

The best part is, you don't have to save it just for your Zoom calls! You can use an anonymous word-cloud generator like Poll Everywhere, or a class-wide Google form. This also works as a lightning-fast, in-person warm-up to the start of each new day in your physical classroom.

---

10 Betsy Mikel, "How Brené Brown Runs Emotionally Intelligent Zoom Meetings," Inc.com, April 15, 2020, inc.com/betsy-mikel/how-brene-brown-runs-emotionally-intelligent-zoom -meetings.html.

BLACKOUT POETRY SHINES
A LIGHT IN THE DARKNESS

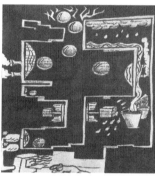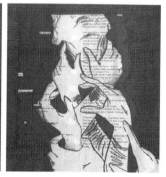

A Fully Engaged Upgrade to simple close reading activities where students will be scouring an assigned text for the main idea.

What if we told you that you could find secret messages locked inside every one of the most famous works of literature, historical writings, or even course textbooks? Now if we handed you a photocopy of a single page, could you discover the deeper meaning hidden within?

See these stunning examples of student artwork? Take a closer look and you'll discover that they're the work of students digging for deeper themes that lie beneath the surface of the poem "Daddy" by Sylvia Plath. Powerful stuff, huh?! This quick game-like approach for deep reading works for any course or content area and can turn hitting those essential main-idea and domain-related standard chores into a challenge, easy as 1-2-3.

All you'll need for this activity is a bag of dice and a black magic marker.

STEP ONE: Tell students that their goal is to reveal the deeper meaning hidden within the original work. To find it, they'll have to cross out all the words on the page that they believe are not important to conveying its central idea. Once they've crossed out all the extra words, they'll create a brand new poem or very short story using only the remaining words.

STEP TWO: Have each student roll a bag of seven role playing-game dice (you know, the funny shaped ones that folks use to play Dungeons & Dragons!) and add up whatever total is shown. That total is now their magic number (we'll call this "X"). Once each student has their magic number, ask them to circle *only* the X words that they think are the most important in the original work, crossing out everything else on the page. They'll need to read closely! Because, as with Brené Brown's two-word warm-up, there's a cap on the number of words they're allowed to use.

STEP THREE: Have each student use a magic marker to black out everything else on their printed page. And when they're done, ask them to find inspiration from the remaining words to draw a picture that illustrates the "hidden" main idea of the original work from which those words were excerpted.

That's it. For any story, poem, historical document, or online article you can think of. No need for simulations. No "role playing." And no "battling" with rival players in an effort to knock the other guy down on your quest to be the best. Just a serious effort to make sense of a challenging text. Simply roll the dice and unlock the mystery that awaits you inside the printed page. All made possible by a single gamification design principle: the voluntary attempt to overcome one unnecessary obstacle.

HOW GAMES HELP PLAYERS
FEEL DRAWN TOGETHER

One of the most appealing things about games is how easily they can welcome new players of all ages, backgrounds, colors, and creeds to the table. Every four years, the world pays rapt attention as the Olympic Games invites athletes from around the globe to a sporting spectacle with roots dating all the way back to Ancient Greece. But it's not just the Ancient Greeks who got in on the gaming fun! Some of the oldest games on earth, like mancala, originate from the fourth century in Egypt and other parts of Africa, and historians generally concur that the timeless game of chess was invented way back in the sixth century in India.

Games are timeless and universal. Each time we sit back down at the table, we join in a community of players that welcomes entire generations of people from all around the world.

Perhaps this is the best part of playful pedagogy: Games don't care whether you're black or white, rich or poor, gay or straight. When the game begins, everyone is welcome.

WHEN THE GAME BEGINS, EVERYONE IS WELCOME.

Games are, by nature, inclusive. So what might it look like if your students were asked to see themselves as a "character" inside the "game" world of the content that you have just learned together in class? For an assignment like this one, students can illustrate key concepts from your current unit of study as if they were action-figure playsets, collectable trading-card series, brightly colored comic books, or full-blown video games. If you want to add a tactile twist, your students can even build the "world" of what you're studying out of LEGO bricks, 3-D printers, or digital creation tools like *Minecraft*—then take photos or video of their creations and post short explainer walkthroughs of how and why they decided to include whichever particular details ultimately made it into their creation.

Once you start playing with imagination, the possibilities are literally endless.

So let's close out this chapter by taking one more look at what a fully engaged classroom might look like if we can put the power of play to work to punch up some really serious learning. Zero advance prep required. Any course or content area. Just push play.

TRANSFORM RESEARCH INTO
A REVOLUTION

A Fully Engaged Upgrade to research projects requiring citations

What if Netflix decided to film an exclusive series devoted entirely to your current unit of study?

Can you capture the world's attention with a binge-worthy series that will get people talking about major real-life issues? Rather than making light of trauma or forcing students to reenact the role of oppressed persons or their oppressors, this gamified twist on a tough topic turns your classes into small groups of competing production crews. Simply divide your students into rival teams and provide them with a slideshow template like the one pictured above. Then have them work with their teammates to imagine what your current unit of study might look like if it was a binge-worthy docuseries.

Suddenly your classroom is alive with energy and wonder as students start scouring the web for the perfect images, videos, and original content to include in their episode summaries. And since they know there's a rival "production crew" out there vying for potential viewers, they're willing to work *that much harder* to create a cohesive slideshow that is clean, professional, and polished from every angle.

This simple tweak turns content consumers into content creators and keeps your curriculum at the center of the action at every stage of play. Eustress kicks into overdrive as students springboard from the familiar world of streaming service to start conducting research into even the most challenging corners of your subject matter. Whether you use this for an end-of-unit recap, a basic five-paragraph essay outline, or something as daunting as an annotated bibliography, it's an outstanding way to elicit serious levels of self-actualization and esteem.

This activity can be repurposed for any course, content area, or grade level—including when you're dealing with lighter topics. Using the familiar Netflix-like interface takes the sting out of self-paced research, and by having students embed relevant websites, photos, and video links throughout the presentation, they'll have created a visually stunning digital presentation that can be used to pre-teach (or re-teach) any topic you can think of.

NEXT-LEVEL PEDAGOGY AWAITS

From the shapeshifting secrets of the Starman to the student-centered streaming service, the examples outlined in this chapter are just a sneak preview of the sort of joyful, playful pedagogy of wonder and excitement that lives inside of the Timeless Temple of the Fully Engaged classroom. Congratulations! You are now the proud owner of a long-lost map to guide you toward our game-changing goal. And with these rock solid foundations of play now firmly under our feet, we are that much closer to unlocking countless treasures that await us on the journey ahead. The only problem? The Timeless Temple just so happens to be located somewhere on the farthest shores of the Legendary Lake of Learning.

So it looks like we're all going for a deeper dive.

Questions for Discussion

David Bowie believed that there were two stars in rock 'n' roll, the performer and the audience, and his constant reinvention at each stage of the game was always marked by a finger placed firmly on the pulse of his fans. What are some of the ch-ch-changes that your students might be going through? How might the unique needs of this year's students differ from those of students whom you may have encountered in years past?

The Christmas Truce is a real-life story of historical enemies finding common bonds through the shared appreciation of one another's humanity. Have you ever found yourself experiencing growth during a time of adversity? See if you can trace your own story up each of the tiers of Maslow's hierarchy of needs.

Consent is the foundation of any good game. And classroom teachers have a responsibility never to create lesson plans that traumatize or trivialize a person's real-life distress. Think back to a time when you may have experienced distress in your own life. Now compare that to a time when you experienced eustress. What differences do you notice?

CHAPTER TWO

FOUR SECRETS OF DEEPER LEARNING

It's dangerous to go alone! Take this.

—The Legend of Zelda

Ciao, everyone! It's Michael. I have been a teacher and learner all over this world. From my studies in Korea and Rome, to my teaching in Milan and Milwaukee, to that time I unexpectedly found myself running with the bulls in Pamplona (that's a story for another time!), my educational philosophy can best be summed up by a Cesare Pavese quote: "We don't remember days, we remember moments." I think educators can and should draw from their own passions from life outside of the classroom to create moment-filled classes that can literally change the trajectory of our students' lives. And when we do it right, we really can change the world!

So in this chapter, we're going to borrow a few "epic moment" tricks from one of our favorite adventures of all time to see if we can't help you lock in some serious learning with a playful twist. We really want this stuff to be memorable.

Let's face it: studying the finer points of educational philosophy can be a total slog.

Sure, there are the rare few of us out there who name drop John Dewey or geek out about Maria Montessori and Jean Piaget. But we're not in graduate school anymore, Toto. Black-and-white academic theory is all well and good for textbooks. But today's educators don't have time for navel-gazing white papers when we are living in the vibrant world of real-life teaching technicolor! We need epic stories. Colorful characters. And action-packed strategies that will make our lesson plans work better today!

Sounds like the perfect time for us to go on an adventure.

In this chapter, you'll move through a hero's quest story like The Legend of Zelda to show you how deep all this gamification stuff can really go. And with a few clever game-inspired gems waiting for you to discover along the way, we'd like to present some serious research by way of some superpowered storytelling of our own. As we'll soon see, the human memory is hardwired to respond really well to the lasting impressions from a well-told story.

FULLY ENGAGED HERO'S QUEST: FIND THE FOUR SECRETS OF THE DEEP

Picture yourself standing on the sun-soaked shores of a vast body of water. This is the Lake of Learning—and it's even wider than the stories had led you to believe! Legend tells us that somewhere across the surface of these swirling waters lies a Timeless Temple of the Fully Engaged Classroom.

Our guide map has already revealed to us the foundation upon which this temple was once built. We must sail to each of the four corners of these mythic waters to recover the Secrets of the Deeper Learning—a series of ancient artifacts that, when combined, have the power to help us gain lifetime access to this legendary structure.

Your challenge: recover all four Secrets of Deeper Learning, combine their teaching powers, and gain lifetime access to the Timeless Temple of the Fully Engaged Classroom!

Seeing yourself at the center of an unfolding story helps to maintain a clearer picture of progress toward a goal that grows ever closer with each breath you take. The pleasure centers of your brain flood with all sorts of chemicals more potent than whatever potions might be sold in any apothecary. Momentum pulls you forward so you want to learn more. And research suggests that you are already *that much more likely* to read on *and that much more likely to remember what you've read* now that you see yourself at the heart of all the action.

Behold, the power of storytelling! This chapter offers highlights from nearly a century's worth of academic scholarship to support all the factors that will help you develop a fully engaged classroom, each of which is presented here as its very own bite-sized installment of a larger adventure story. Let's dive in!

THE FIRST SECRET OF DEEPER LEARNING: A TALE OF TWO HEROES

We'll start in the shallow end of the research pool by following the daring exploits of a pair of explorers who first braved these same waters of engagement nearly forty years ago.

The first is the tale of an intrepid jungle explorer named Pitfall Harry.

Released in 1982, Atari's *Pitfall* was one of the biggest video games of its era. In *Pitfall*, the story is pretty straightforward: players control our hero (Pitfall Harry), guiding him through a maze-like jungle and dodging all sorts of enemies, including snakes, scorpions, and pits of quicksand. There's not much else to the game's storyline. And you get the hang of the basic "don't fall in the pit" gameplay: the whole thing takes about twenty minutes to beat from start to finish. Perhaps unsurprisingly, this adventure didn't age so well as games became increasingly complex. And before long, both Pitfall Harry and his parent company, Atari, ultimately joined countless other video game titles in that great arcade in the sky.

Now let's compare the story of *Pitfall* to another 8-bit adventure that was released just four years later. The hero of this franchise? A pint-sized pixie named Link.

We're talking, of course, about *The Legend of Zelda*—a title that has gone on to become a cornerstone of the Nintendo franchise, spawning over two dozen sequels, providing gamers with billions of hours of playing time, and netting the company well over one hundred million individual copies sold. The original Zelda game moved a respectable six million units—right on par with the original *Pitfall*'s success from back in the day. But the latest installment in the Zelda series? As of this writing, 2017's *Breath of the Wild* has sold—get this—more than nineteen million copies and counting.[1] So how the heck did they pull this off?

When you stack the original *Pitfall* up against *The Legend of Zelda*, there aren't so many major differences on paper. Graphics? Comparable. Controls? Equally intuitive for both games. Average time required to complete the entire game from start to finish? *Pitfall:* Less than twenty minutes. *The Legend of Zelda:* About eight-and-a-half hours.

Whoa. Hang on a second.

Pitfall has exactly one trick to its credit: run forward and try not to fall down the holes. *The Legend of Zelda*, meanwhile, offers hundreds of opportunities for our diminutive hero to strike up conversations, solve challenges, and collect hard-to-find items from and for all sorts of colorful strangers who inhabit the mysterious land of Hyrule. It's, like, really stinking hard. On purpose. And even though the game is infinitely more challenging than *Pitfall*, we can't wait to learn what it has to teach us through the infinitely controllable "Link" between the players of the game and its young hero.

James Paul Gee is widely regarded as one of the world's foremost experts on the intersection between gaming and education. In his 2007 book *What Video Games Have to Teach Us about Learning and Literacy*,

---

1 *"The Legend of Zelda,"* Video Game Sales Wiki, last modified June 17, 2021, vgsales.fandom .com/wiki/The_Legend_of_Zelda.

Gee explains the unlikely reason that really hard video games like *The Legend of Zelda* seem to succeed:

> So here we have something that is long, hard, and challenging. However, you cannot play a game if you cannot learn it. If no one plays a game, it does not sell, and the company that makes it goes broke. Of course, designers could keep making the games shorter and simpler to facilitate learning. That's often what schools do. But no, in this case, game designers keep making the games longer and more challenging (and introduce new things in new ones) and still manage to get them learned. How?
>
> If you think about it, you see a Darwinian sort of thing going on here. If a game, for whatever reason, has good principles of learning built into its design—that is, if it facilitates learning in good ways—then it gets played and can sell a lot of copies, if it is otherwise good as well. If a game has poor learning principles built into its design, then it won't get learned or played and it won't sell well. In the end, then, video games represent a process, thanks to what Marx calls the 'creativity of capitalism,' that leads to better and better designs for good learning and, indeed, good learning of hard and challenging things.[2]

The Legend of Zelda is a textbook example of the perfectly made video game franchise. Its scope is daunting, far beyond the difficulty level of its contemporaries, and each new installment in the franchise is even more sprawling and ambitious than the last. But it always places the learner squarely behind the eyes of the hero. We follow Link through all sorts of uncharted landscapes as we learn to "Look! Listen!" to the fairies and woodland sprites that offer him guidance along the way. And without our hero ever speaking so much as a word, we grow

---

2 James Paul Gee, *What Video Games Have to Teach Us about Learning and Literacy* (New York: St. Martin's Griffin, 2003).

deeply invested in the game, to the point where we are ultimately able to showcase a rich and diverse skill set as it tests our timing, accuracy, and critical thinking abilities while Link unlocks all sorts of new power-up items to help him along his never-ending journey.

Hey! That reminds us: Dr. Gee's insight has just helped us find a shiny new discovery of our own.

> **The First Secret of Deeper Learning:** Great games actually make us excited to work harder. But can our classrooms say the same?

THE SECOND SECRET OF DEEPER LEARNING: ARISTOTLE IN THE ROOM WHERE IT HAPPENS

Reassured by the rush of dopamine that comes from discovering new things, we sail away from the familiar shores of the Game of School and into the deeper waters of institutional reform. But we're certainly not the first young, scrappy, and hungry upstarts to tell the world that a system is in serious need of a revolution.

Perhaps you've heard of Alexander Hamilton?

At the White House's Evening of Poetry, Music, and the Spoken Word on May 12, 2009, a relatively little-known playwright named Lin-Manuel Miranda took the stage and debuted the first song of what was, at the time, still a "concept album" he'd been working on in the months leading up to the event. The album was about the life of America's first treasury secretary, Alexander Hamilton. Miranda explained his fascination with Hamilton, noting how in spite of the fact that the man "was born a penniless orphan in St. Croix of illegitimate birth, [Hamilton] became George Washington's right-hand man, became Treasury Secretary, caught beef with every other Founding Father . . . all on the strength of his writing." And in a sentiment that would soon become prophetic for the trajectory of his own career, Miranda added, "I think he embodies words' ability to make a difference."

When the composer revealed that he was about to tell the story of this two-hundred-years-dead Founding Father in a hip-hop song, the crowd—including President Barack Obama and First Lady Michelle Obama—couldn't help but snicker at the idea. As President Obama later remarked at the 70th Annual Tony Awards, "I confess, we all laughed. But who's laughing now?"

One would be hard pressed to disagree.

Miranda's unlikely concept album went on to become a full-blown Broadway musical and a cultural juggernaut. Netting upward of half a billion dollars in domestic box-office revenue, *Hamilton* captured the acclaim of audiences and critics alike. Miranda went on to be awarded the 2016 Pulitzer Prize for Drama and a 2016 MacArthur Foundation "Genius" Grant, and the record-breaking show netted eleven Tony Awards. Michelle Obama even welcomed the entire cast of *Hamilton* to the White House in May of 2016. She raved about the show, telling audiences, "It was simply, as I tell everybody, the best piece of art in any form that I have ever seen in my life."

Today, it's likely that most every student in the United States is at least familiar to some degree with the story of America's first treasury secretary. As President Obama himself concluded, "Hamilton has become not only a smash hit, but a civics lesson our kids can't get enough of. One with fierce, youthful energy. One where rap is the language of revolution [and] hip hop, its urgent soundtrack."

By taking a bold risk, keeping a finger planted firmly on the pulse of its audience, and putting a fresh take on a timeless story, Lin-Manuel Miranda's *Hamilton* helped students find a passion for social studies in the most unlikely of places.

But perhaps this is no surprise. In the opening lines of his *Metaphysics*, Aristotle argues: "All men by nature desire to know. An indication of this is the delight we take in our senses; for even apart from their usefulness they are loved for themselves; and above all others the sense of sight."

In layman's terms: "Look around, look around, at how lucky we are to be alive right now."

Aristotle argues that it is human nature to seek knowledge for its own sake. Not for extrinsic rewards, but for intrinsic delight of the senses. *Hamilton* tapped into the self-made ethos of the hip-hop generation to help students see themselves in the story of America's Founding Fathers. And while students weren't worrying themselves about what grades they might be getting on all this newfound knowledge about the American Revolution, they quietly went about memorizing all 20,520 words in the show. That's more words than are spoken in nine of Shakespeare's plays, including *A Midsummer Night's Dream* (16,511), *Macbeth* (17,121), and *Julius Caesar* (19,703).

When a person is captivated, they don't need to be held captive.

The research bears this out. Time and again, contemporary behaviorist researchers like *New York Times* best-selling author Daniel Pink and Stanford psychologist Carol Dweck find themselves returning to the same Aristotelian conclusion: extrinsic rewards are overrated. People hunger for autonomy. They yearn for authentic purpose. And they are fueled by the desire to master a quest of their own choosing. Control leads to compliance; autonomy leads to engagement.[3]

We don't do this stuff for grades.

Once our brains find something that we truly love (like a great tune by our favorite band), we immediately find ourselves humming right along and wanting to learn more. So whether you're staring at the ruins of the Acropolis or standing inside "The Room Where it Happens" for your favorite Broadway performance, the sheer beauty of what lies before you immediately sends your brain flooding with positive endorphins. You feel overcome by a sense of awe at just how much time and thought must have gone into breathing life into this

---

3   Daniel Pink, *Drive: The Surprising Truth About What Motivates Us* (New York: Riverhead Books, 2009).

elaborate and well-made thing, and you can't wait to learn everything there is to know about it.

Real learning isn't necessarily designed to be easy. But it is supposed to be fun.

The Second Secret of Deeper Learning: Great games invite us to delight in our senses, learning what we want, when we want, and how we want to. Is that the story of our schools? If not: *What's stopping us?*

THE THIRD SECRET OF DEEPER LEARNING: A MAGICAL CHAIN AND A FREE CARWASH

The next stop in our dive through the Lake of Learning leads us to a game-changing discovery from 1922, when a bright young Russian psychologist named Bluma Zeigarnik (1901–1988) was the first researcher to take serious note of the way the human brain responds to unfinished tasks. Her interest in the phenomenon didn't develop as the product of decades spent in the lab—she actually stumbled upon it in a café. As researchers from the world-famous think tank the Gottman Institute explain:

> Watching waiters in a café in Vienna, Bluma realized something very strange in their behavior: they only seemed to remember the orders that they were in the process of serving. As soon as they had completed their task, the orders disappeared from their memory. What Bluma didn't realize were the implications of her findings.
>
> "The Ziegarnik Effect," in simple terms, is the propensity of human beings to remember uncompleted or interrupted tasks better than completed tasks.[4]

---

4 Ellie Lisitsa, "The Zeigarnik Effect," Gottman Relationship Blog, Gottman Institute, August 15, 2012, gottman.com/blog/what-makes-love-last-the-zeigarnik-effect/.

In short, the momentary distress caused in our brain each time it is made aware of an incomplete task actually makes us hyperfixate on that unfinished business all the more. It's the reason why we wake up in the middle of the night freaking out over unsent thank you cards from two weeks ago. Or why we can't wait to get back to that next chapter of a really good book. It also helps explain why video games just so happen to post a prominently visible high score right there at the top of the screen.

The brain kicks into overdrive at the thought of a task that still requires our attention. And when we feel closer to finishing it, we kick that much harder to see things through to completion.

Now let's flash forward a century or so and head to our friendly neighborhood retailer to see how modern psychologists have taken the Ziegarnik effect to the next level in their understanding of human behavior. Have you ever received one of those customer-loyalty cards where you collect stamps or hole punches to score a free sandwich or a car wash, one step at a time? In the March 2006 issue of the *Journal of Customer Research*, Joseph Nunes from the University of Southern California's Marshall School of Business and Xavier Dreze from the Wharton School at the University of Pennsylvania published a fascinating study on the subject.[5] What they found is a brilliant psychological sleight of hand.

It's called the endowed-progress effect. And it works like a charm. Here's what the researchers discovered: Over the course of two Saturdays in June, two different groups of customers at a local car wash were randomly given a total of three hundred loyalty cards. One group was given a loyalty card with eight blank squares. The other group was given a loyalty card with ten squares—the first two of which were automatically stamped for them as freebies. Both groups were then told that they'd receive a free car wash if they were able to collect enough stamps to complete their card. But by the time the study was over nine

---

5 Joseph Nunes and Xavier Dreze, "The Endowed Progress Effect: How Artificial Advancement Increases Effort," *Journal of Consumer Research* 32 (March 2006): 504–512, papers.ssrn.com/sol3/papers.cfm?abstract_id=991962.

months later, the second group had completed stamps for each of the remaining squares on their card at a jaw-dropping rate of 82 percent higher than the first group!

The trick of it all? Both groups had effectively been handed cards with 8 squares left to complete. But once you start seeing yourself making progress (even if the books are cooked to help you get that initial boost of momentum), you're that much more likely to continue moving forward.

It's the same reason why casinos will offer guests $100 in free chips just for showing up. Why video games like *World of Warcraft* provide players with a clear visual checklist of all the missions they've completed to date. Why board games like Pandemic have a sort of "doomsday clock" mechanism built in, where all players are constantly aware that the game is only just a few turns away from reaching its final round.

It's also why we decided to scatter all of these heady philosophical lessons through an easily tracked four-point treasure hunt across the waters of the Legendary Lake of Learning. Which reminds us . . .

> **The Third Secret of Deeper Learning:** Through simple visuals like mini maps and progress meters, well-designed games help make learning visible. When we see signs of progress, we feel smarter and stronger. But what visual signs of growth do students have in the traditional classroom aside from an abstract and often arbitrary system of letter grades?

THE FOURTH SECRET OF DEEPER LEARNING: PRIBRAM'S SUNSHINE AND THE STORIES THAT LAST A LIFETIME

The truth is, the average human brain is constantly being bombarded with all sorts of information all at once. In fact, Hungarian-born physicist and mathematician John von Neumann (1903–1957) once calculated that, over the course of the average human lifetime, the brain stores 2.8 x 1020 (280,000,000,000,000,000,000) bits of information.[6] That's an awful lot of chances to forget what we've just learned.

But the faster we can crystalize a whole bunch of new information (say, into a mnemonic device, or a handy acronym, or into a singular epic story with clearly defined beats along the way), the more likely we are to remember it. Just Ask My Dear Aunt Sally. Or think back to that time My Very Educated Mother Just Served Us Nine Pickles.

Believe it or not: those simple stories can last a lifetime.

In the 2004 science fiction romance *Eternal Sunshine of the Spotless Mind*, a heartbroken hero (played by Jim Carrey) heads to a local medical facility to undergo a radical new treatment that promises to wipe away every trace of his memories from a failed relationship with his former flame (played by Kate Winslet). It's a novel prospect: pay a few bucks to spend an evening under the knife, and poof! All those sad stories of the one that got away are wiped clean forever. Of course, this doesn't quite work out the way our hero thought it would. And when we dig a little deeper into the past century or so of real-life brain research, it turns out that what we're learning from the field of neuropsychology doesn't work out quite that way, either.

Karl Pribram (1919–2015) was the founder of a branch of neuroscience known as *holonomic brain theory*, a fascinating branch of quantum consciousness that basically suggests that specific memories in the human brain are not simply preserved in any one particular physical location like individual books lying on the shelves. When it comes to memory, Pribram suggests, the brain works more like a giant hologram: each piece of the brain actually contains enough storytelling power to reconstruct every bit of the whole thread. Over the course of his life's work, Pribram detailed case after case where even people with medical conditions who had to have a portion of their brains surgically removed were not shown to exhibit loss of specific memories. Though

---

6 Message to Eagle, "Our Brain Is a Holographic Machine Existing in a Holographic Universe," April 9, 2014, messagetoeagle.com/our-brain-is-a-holographic-machine-existing-in-a -holographic-universe.

different hemispheres of the brain could indeed be connected to everything ranging from particular fine motor skills to specific centers that govern behavioral traits, Pribram and his team consistently found that no matter what portion of the brain was removed, a person's memories simply could not be eradicated.

In essence, our brains are hardwired for storytelling. It's the reason why we can watch countless episodes of multiple TV programs over the course of the same weekend and never once mix up the characters from *The Office* with the storylines from *Schitt's Creek*. It explains why we can drift off to sleep with our favorite book on the nightstand beside us and can't wait to dive right back into the action the moment we wake up the next morning. And it's why Hollywood blockbusters can draw millions of fans to the theaters with little more than a movie trailer containing the phrase, "In a world where . . . "

Our brains flood with the prospect of millions of possibilities as we connect that which is new to memories of things we've already enjoyed. It's exciting. It's enticing. And it's addictive in the best way possible.

Sure, individual facts, dates, and figures can get lost along the way. But when we create memories by synthesizing new stories with the old, something incredible happens. Our neural pathways start firing on all cylinders as these new lessons begin attaching themselves to countless other tales already woven through the rich tapestry of our minds. And before we know it, we've got memories that are instantly wired in a million different directions throughout our entire brain as a whole.

Stories are sticky. And that's exactly why they work.

The Fourth Secret of Deeper Learning: The human brain is built for stories. How can we weave larger thematic stories throughout our daily lessons to transform rote memorization exercises into enriched springboards for deeper comprehension?

BEHOLD THE TIMELESS TEMPLE OF THE FULLY ENGAGED CLASSROOM!

If the first two chapters of this book were heavy on the "why" of playful pedagogy, then the remainder of our journey will feature a myriad of "how" and "what" examples of what these same underlying principles look like when put into play inside a classrooms. From here on out, we're hitting the ground running with concrete examples and practical strategies. Think of these next four chapters as equally sized "Pillars of Playful Learning" to support a final chapter—a "roof" under which people and purpose find their home in a classroom that is fully engaged. Each chapter will offer the building blocks for how to borrow ideas for your teaching practice from a specific array of student engagement strategies. But keep in mind: while these activities are powerful "bricks" for a classroom where every learner is fully engaged, it's up to teachers to facilitate and serve as the "mortar" that binds these instructional practices together with empathy, compassion, and student-centered intentionality. We think you'll find these "how-to" blueprints incredibly helpful as you become the architects of classroom experiences of your own that can be truly transformational for every learner who steps foot inside these hallowed halls.

Now let's get to building!

Questions for Discussion

We opened this chapter by geeking out over *The Legend of Zelda*! But what game do you love? Think of a board game, sport, or video game that you really enjoy, and see how it stacks up with each of the four Secrets of Deeper Learning. How does the game that you selected:

- Offer increasing levels of challenge to invite you to play it again and again?
- Appeal to your senses through its aesthetic elements of sight and sound?
- Provide you feedback that you're "oh so close!"?
- Help you get caught up in a story to find yourself "in a world where . . . "?

Consider trying this step-by-step debrief exercise with your friends or family members after playing a board game from your closet!

Take one more look at the examples of the four Secrets of Deeper Learning we encountered in this chapter:

- A video game that makes us genuinely excited to work harder
- A Broadway musical that invites us to join a learning revolution
- A car wash promotion that convinces us we're *so close* to a reward
- A motion picture that tells us a story we simply can't forget

How can you incorporate any of the powerful lessons that come from these Secrets of Deeper Learning into the lesson-planning process for your own classroom?

Do you have any lingering questions before you enter the Timeless Temple of the Fully Engaged Classroom? Let us know on Twitter by sending a message to @MrMatera or @MeehanEDU. And use that hashtag #EMC2Learning. We're here to help!

CHAPTER THREE

CHOICE AND CHALLENGE

Salt has a greater impact on flavor than any other ingredient. Learn to use it well, and food will taste good.

—Samin Nosrat

You want in on a little secret? Life is better when you're eating good food with good people. Growing up in a split Italian/Irish household I (Michael) saw firsthand the importance of hospitality and the power that food has to create memories and happy moments. I mean, we all remember with vivid detail our family's specialty dishes, don't we? You know the ones I'm talking about.

Some of you may know that I love cooking and am a self-proclaimed foodie. Now, we foodies get a bad rap and are sometimes labeled as snobs, so let me set the record straight: Snobs are snobs, foodies are foodies. They don't have to be one to be the other. I will take a good comfort-food dish or yummy casserole any day! A true foodie has a passion for the table. They love the shared experiences, the many challenges and choices that are discussed and decided upon around that table. There is an old Italian expression "A tavola non si invecchia"—which translates to "You don't get old at the table." This saying encapsulates that beating heart of a foodie. With good company and good food, time doesn't pass. You could spend hours gathered together and not a moment will be wasted.

As a single father, one of my greatest joys is meal time with my daughter, Mila. At the table, we talk about our roses and thorns for the day. We even talk about our hopeful wishes for tomorrow. We call those our rose buds. But the foodie in me was most delighted when my daughter began to express interest in learning how to cook. She wants to be a passionate foodie who loves to pick out the right ingredient, master some dishes that delight our guests, and most humbly feel the warmth in her heart when she shares a morsel with someone she loves.

Learning to cook and discover the joy of food takes time. There are so many choices—and yes, even challenges—to overcome along the way. My daughter began joining me in the kitchen at four years old. Just keeping her on her stool was a big challenge, let alone the idea of exposing her to different ingredients. Over the years she has continued to expand her palate by trying new things. When she helps me create a dish, I ask her to try the ingredients separately. When we made our first chocolate chip cookie recipe she excitedly tried each ingredient one at a time. The sugar? No problem! The raw vanilla extract? Eww. Not the best. But the showstopper was when I told her we added salt to the cookies. She couldn't believe that this ingredient made it into her perfect chocolate chip cookie!

Having her try each of the ingredients separately showed Mila that, in the end, an artful combination of these flavors and textures creates something unique and oh-so-delicious. With each new recipe, she deepens her understanding of how to use salt as an enhancer. A pinch in the pan, a dash over the final dish or even a salty marinade that allows flavor to permeate the thickest cut of meat. Mila has chosen to step up to many culinary challenges in our kitchen, from homemade pizza dough to a tasty bruschetta that rivals any Roman ristorante—this girl can cook!

Many of the best family chefs say that the secret ingredient to all good cooking is love. Of course, the truth is that love is . . . not actually an ingredient. A good chef is not adding love to the dish, but they are making that dish with loved ones in mind. It's a subtle shift, but an important one to understand. Do we put our heart into our work? No question! And we as the chefs of our classroom need to remember to keep our students in mind as we create educational dishes for them to devour and remember. Making things with love is essential. But love itself isn't an ingredient.

Salt, however, is.

Salt is a flavor enhancer. Some educators say that they shouldn't have to dress up their lessons with engagement strategies. You might have even heard these folks tossing around the analogy that these techniques are nothing more than "edutainment" or "chocolate-covered broccoli," and that all we're doing is smothering the good stuff under a sugary veneer. In short, they're saying that there is no need for them to spend their time on this. The chocolate is there to cover up, hide, or distract our peewee patrons from the healthy veggies. In effect, the skeptic serves up a big old plate of new content knowledge and tells students to "eat your broccoli." But remember, the secret of being a good chef is remembering the loved ones you are cooking for.

With this new frame of reference, using engagement strategies isn't chocolate-covered broccoli, but instead, it is the salt in our lessons. Not there to cover up and distract, but rather to enhance the flavors of the lesson, to bring out the richness of the experience, and to create a savory moment. When someone imparts the right amount of salt in a dish made for their loved ones, both their hearts warm up with the true intrinsic lesson of love. The message is loud and clear: "You made this for me!"

Mangia!

THE LEGACY OF MATH BLASTER

Eric Klopfer knows a thing or two about serving up some serious substance with a dash of fun. When he's not busy working as a professor and director of the Scheller Teacher Education Program and the Education Arcade at MIT, Klopfer is also an educational game designer. His work explores how playful pedagogy like educational technology, games, and computer simulations can be tools for teaching complex systems and developing cognitive and computational thinking skills. We're not talking *Oregon Trail* or *Reader Rabbit* here, gang. Klopfer's work is light years beyond those early computer titles that used an appetizing shell to obscure otherwise flavorless course content.

Klopfer takes issue with the fact that so many educational games ask players to simply answer subject-specific questions which unlock the chance to play a mini-game reward. A classic low-tech example: a teacher peppers their class with a series of review questions for a big upcoming test. And every time a student answers a question right, they are rewarded with the opportunity to shoot a crumpled up piece of paper into a small basketball hoop at the front of the class.

Entertaining? Big time.

Challenging? Sure . . . if you're teaching a physical education class.

But is it providing an authentic opportunity to engage more deeply with the course content? Not so much. Yes, it's a fun distraction, but it's not what we mean by asking teachers to craft playful lesson plans that offer choice and challenge. Klopfer calls this trend the "Legacy of *Math Blaster*"—named after the famous educational computer game from the early 1980s. Solve a math problem, and you get the chance to fire a shot at an asteroid in the sky. The only problem? There's nothing inherently "mathy" about the connection between solving basic addition or subtraction questions and earning the chance to take a shot at an asteroid. The game could just as easily be played with chemistry equations, history timelines, or low-level trivia related to famous recording artists.

For teachers, that's a bad thing. This disjointed fun-and-games approach inadvertently leaves a subtle but lingering disconnect for our students. Before long, they start to draw the line between the hard stuff (the subject matter) and the fun stuff (the asteroid blasting). Klopfer calls this phenomenon "edutainment," where the play is the reward for learning. [1] And in the long run, many of these kinds of "sweet reward" style games ultimately end up causing more harm than good.

In other words, the paper basketball example is a *Math Blaster*-like game with a sugary shell that has no substance. Consequently, your proverbial "chocolate-covered broccoli" actually ends up teaching your students that shooting baskets (the chocolate) is crazy fun. But solving problems that are actually related to your content (the broccoli) is still a tough one to swallow.

When we're talking about providing authentic choice and challenge in our fully engaged classrooms, we need to be less chocolate and more salt. Our playful pedagogy should help to enrich the flavor of all the good stuff before us. So the question is not simply "What can I do to make my course content fun?" But rather, what do people really enjoy about this subject matter? And how do we amplify it and show that to them?

THE TRICK WAS TO SURRENDER TO THE FLOW

Here's the good news: You already love the subject you're teaching (at least we hope so)! And so you've got a lifetime's worth of excitement for your content that's just waiting to make its way into your lesson planning. So how do you create a game-like experience that keeps players firmly "in the zone"?

You'll simply have to go with the flow.

---

1 Eric Klopfer, "Chocolate-Covered Broccoli and Educational Games" (webinar excerpt), Abdul Latif Jameel World Education Lab, MIT, jwel.mit.edu/assets/video/chocolate-covered-broccoli-and-educational-games-webinar-excerpt.

Hungarian-American psychologist Mihaly Csikszentmihalyi is the preeminent scholar in the field of positive psychology. He has spent the past fifty years changing the research game at such noted institutions as the University of Chicago, Lake Forest College, and Claremont Graduate University. The author or coauthor of hundreds of psychological studies and more than two dozen full-length books, Csikszentmihalyi is perhaps most famous for being the first in his field to recognize the psychological concept of "flow." Colloquially, you might have heard this phenomenon described as being "in the zone."

Csikszentmihalyi describes the *flow state* as "the mental state of operation in which a person performing an activity is fully immersed in a feeling of energized focus, full involvement, and enjoyment in the process of the activity."[2] Here's a visual representation of the flow state:

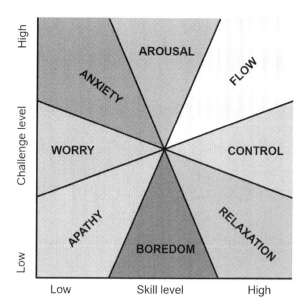

As Csikszentmihalyi explains, this aspirational state of peak performance comes in the sweet spot where a learner's skill level is equally as high as the challenge level that he or she is encountering. Even

---

2 Mihaly Csikszentmihalyi, *Flow: The Psychology of Optimal Experience* (New York: Harper & Row, 1990).

better: they feel themselves getting incrementally stronger as the challenge escalates throughout the game.

What if a student is thrown into the deep end and blindly expected to tackle a challenge well above their ability level? Research suggests they'll experience anxiety or fear that they're simply not up to the task. It's doesn't take much to see how these feelings of self-doubt inform Carol Dweck's research into the world of the difference between having a fixed and a growth mindset. When we run up against an obstacle that's too hard, we immediately become overwhelmed and start to believe that we're neither good enough or smart enough to get the job done.

On the flipside: if the challenge level is too low or the individual too skilled, the student quickly finds themselves bored or apathetic with little reason to take the task seriously. There seems to be little point in bothering when we think we're too smart for a task (one-size-fits-all worksheets, anyone?). So these "too cool for school" students tune the whole thing out just as quickly as their peers tap out from stress.

Like all that wasted porridge in the Three Bears' cabin: Too hot. Too cold.

But in that rare sort of classroom where the learner's belief in their own abilities is ever increasing at the exact same rate as the challenges that lie in their way? That's the Goldilocks spot where everything is *just right*! And that is the flow state in action: a fully engaged world in which the entire activity seems to simultaneously speed up and slow down at the exact same time. It's a state that Csikszentmihalyi describes as *autotelic*—which derives from two Greek words (*auto* meaning "self" and *telos* meaning "goal"). This refers to a self-contained activity, one that is not done with the expectation of some future benefit, but simply because the doing itself is the reward. And it can happen when we're playing a sport, watching our favorite TV show, or simply sharing an afternoon telling stories with family and friends.

It can even happen in the classroom.

In the flow state, we lose ourselves so fully in the task at hand that we'll forget to eat. Forget to sleep or walk the dog. This is the state in which we'll lose entire afternoons binge watching our way through cliffhanging episodes of Netflix or playing video games until—well, we might even roll into work wearing yesterday's clothes.

If we're trying to replicate this addictive, game-like experience in the classroom, it's going to take to take more than a cheap chocolate shell like a fleeting blast at an asteroid or a shot at a basketball hoop. Instead, we have to put a salty spin on the entire infrastructure of our lesson-planning efforts so that we can really bring out the flavor of what makes our course content so appetizing in the first place. And to do it, that means we'll need to design an invisible system of student engagement that perpetually taps into that elusive state of flow.

Chocolate coatings and cotton candy sure are sweet. But we're not here for the fluff, y'all.

So let's get salty!

WELCOME TO THE SAMPLER MENU!

The pages that follow offer a playful collection of gamified twists on everyday classroom activities that can really help bring out the flavor of what makes learning so exciting in the first place.

> You've got plenty of choices here to select from, and if you like the taste of these sample sizes before you, we've got literally hundreds more available on our website at EMC2Learning.com.

These classroom activities can be played individually or in small teams, and we're serving up a baker's dozen to really whet your appetite. So grab one of those tiny plastic spoons and have a bite (or ten—we won't judge)!

Choice Board Bingo

CHOICE BOARD BINGO!

We've just completed another unit of our year-long adventure. Now's your chance to show what you know in any way that you'd like! So would you prefer to keep it "old school" and wrap up this unit with a traditional unit test? Or would you like to take your learning to the next level by using digital tools to create something that other students can learn from? The choice is up to you!

Click on any of the icons to the left to see the detailed assignment guidelines for each of the 25 choices available. How many will you complete by the end of our adventure this year?

A Fully Engaged Upgrade to nightly homework. Can you complete an entire bingo board to show what you know?

Let's Dig In: We're starting with a game-based twist on a classic you've probably seen elsewhere in your teacherly travels. But "choice boards" are a great way to offer students the chance to show what they know in whatever way they feel most comfortable. After all, doesn't writing a quality blog post or a thorough book review demonstrate the same skills that students would otherwise have practiced in a five-paragraph essay?

By turning traditional choice boards into a kind of bingo game, students will immediately recognize the challenge before them: complete any five assignments to fill up their bingo cards by turning in five smaller projects from either the same column, the same row, or on a diagonal. And since you're the one serving up the menu, you can keep all of the writing assignments in a single column. Or put all the tech-friendly assignments, like recording an original podcast or video, in a second. Then, arrange all of the performance-based projects like delivering a short speech or performing an original song about the course content, in a third.

Regardless of which activities make their way into the finished products, students will be choosing from a rich menu *of your creation*! So there's no way they can go wrong. One board, twenty-five different assessment options. And the ability to pop individual challenges in and out at your discretion to test any number of skills.

Annotation Scrambles

 A Fully Engaged Upgrade to tired old text annotation.

Let's Dig In: Remember that forbidden feeling of passing notes to a buddy or your school crush during class back when you were a student? Even if your conversation was completely innocent and you weren't trading answers for an upcoming quiz, it still felt like you were in cahoots with a classmate who was "up to something." Naturally, you did everything in your power to keep these notes hidden from the sight of your unsuspecting teacher. Well, what if we could replicate that same collaborative fun while convincing our students to dig a little deeper into the curriculum at hand?

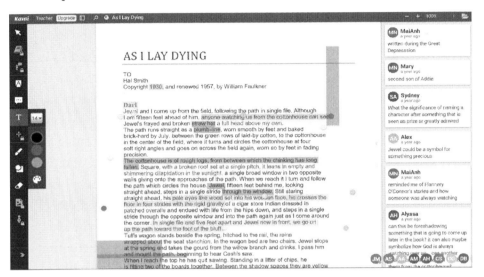

That's why we absolutely love turning tired old note-taking exercises ("open your books to page 391 and take notes on what you've found") into team-vs-team Annotation Scrambles. The game couldn't be any simpler! And if you're in a classroom with one-to-one laptops, free tools like the comment feature in Google Docs or the free PDF-annotation extension called Kami are a great way to spark a vibrant annotation challenge where all students are fully engaged.[3] It's as easy as 1-2-3.

1. Upload a shared document to Kami or to Google Docs and grant all visitors comment access to the unique link that it creates.

2. Share that link with your students, and invite them to go to town with their collaborative annotations—marking up the shared text from their own laptops so that the once black-and-white document starts bursting to life with student comments.

---

3 web.kamihq.com

3. Add a fun team-based twist to your annotation game by dividing your students into two (or three, or four) teams and uploading an additional copy of the same document for each squad. Which team can work together to provide the stronger set of annotations before time expires?

It's often been said that when students turn in work that will only be seen by their teacher, they'll be content with submitting something that's "good enough." But when students submit an assignment that they know will be shared with a larger audience, they have a powerful incentive to turn in something they know will be *good*! Annotating in a group helps students take pride in their collaboration, see that their opinions matter, and learn that the work they're doing is making a real difference in helping their peers work toward the greater good of the group. This helps build connection, community, and the knowledge that the work each individual is doing can make a major impact!

Illustrated Choice Boards

A Fully Engaged Upgrade to breaking students into groups. What secrets are waiting behind each eye-catching photo?

Let's Dig In: Instant intrigue gives way to a team-vs-team challenge of who can discover the deepest secrets! This is a fun way to get students to take a closer look at particular excerpts from an assigned text, and all you'll need is a single slide of an overhead projection and a handful of Post-it Notes.

Fire up your overhead projector with a quick PowerPoint or Google Slides slideshow that contains a massive display of what appears to be a series of unrelated comic book-like panels like the example shown above. Then ask each student to place a Post-it with their name on it directly on top of whichever image most catches their attention. After every student has made their selection (you can even set a limit of no more than X Post-it Notes per image), give a click to the mouse and let each of these photos dissolve one at a time to reveal the assigned sections of an upcoming article (or numbered word problems, or pages of your course textbook, etc.) that correspond with each of these images. The themed photos help offer a clue of what each chunk of the assigned work will be all about, and this small guessing game encourages students to make predictions about how what they're seeing might connect to what they're studying, all with an exciting sense of "drumroll please."

Just like that, students have *that much more* buy-in, ownership, and excitement in having been assigned a chunk of a chapter to present to the class at random. While it accomplishes no functional difference to shuffling out a deck of assignments at random or having students number off by threes or fours, this small tweak lets students feel a sense of ownership in their assigned character or task, helping them start to see this "assignment" as a brief escape into a virtual self and a spark of curiosity to help kickstart their process of discovery.

Graffiti Pages

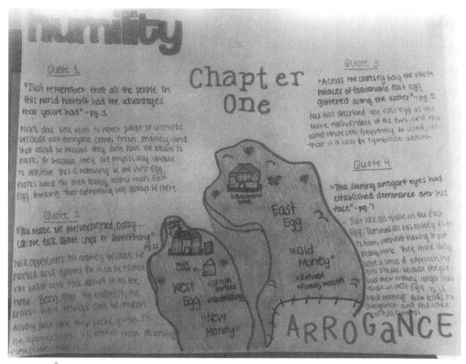

A Fully Engaged Upgrade to traditional "take notes on this chapter" homework assignments.

Let's Dig In: Sketchnoting is a powerful tool in any teacher's playbook. And it doesn't require a lick of artistic ability! This full-color activity can be inserted at any point of a traditional lesson plan (as a warm-up, as homework, or as a refreshing twist on independent work). Even better, it blends creative and analytical thinking, and it all begins with a single blank page.

Simply ask your students to take a blank piece of paper and doodle a bunch of images inspired by what they've just learned. Really: it's that easy. To ratchet up the challenge factor (which makes this deceptively simple technique a perfect strategy for older students), ask students to add a quick caption or annotation with corresponding page numbers from the text to help readers understand just what details, exactly, they've chosen to include in their creation.

The end.

Graffiti pages take this concept to the next level by transforming once-tiny sketchnotes into full-blown works of art like a spray painted mural or tattoo sleeve. The challenge here? Use the front side of an entire sheet of paper to provide an eye-catching visual creation that can help a passerby quickly make sense of a single concept blown out over the course of an entire page. For starters, you might ask students to throw in:

- Two big pictures (about the size of the bottom of a coffee cup), with a quick line or two of annotation or caption beneath them to help explain the image.
- Two giant words that sum up what the student believes to have been the biggest takeaways from the assigned reading. These letters represent those all-important main ideas, so they should be big and bold and pop out from the rest of the smaller details!
- Four direct quotes or lines of significance from the assigned reading—complete with the page number from which this quote was taken. And don't forget to include the attributions for each of these items to help us know who said what!

Graffiti pages add an immediate jolt of life and energy to any lesson plan. They are infinitely scalable and packed with serious potential for brain-dumping at any level. You can ramp up the creativity by asking students to use magic markers, colored pencils, or crayons in their creations to really lock in that multisensory learning. Afterward, you can post and share everyone's submissions in a physical or virtual gallery walk (say, in a shared Google Slides presentation) to help the class strike up a conversation about the big-picture takeaways that the reading might have inspired.

Subject-Matter Sudoku

	HAMLET	LAERTES	CLAUDIUS	OPHELIA	HORATIO	GHOST	GERTRUDE
HAMLET	Haunted by a ghost			Were once madly in love			
LAERTES	Fight one another in a grave-yard						
CLAUDIUS			Killed a king				Got married to one another after the king died
OPHELIA		Children of Polonius					
HORATIO							
GHOST							
GERTRUDE							

A Fully Engaged Upgrade to end-of-unit review activities (sorry, Jeopardy!). Can you complete the entire matrix?

Let's Dig In: Chances are that you've probably tried your hand at putting together a traditional end-of-unit Jeopardy! or Kahoot! review game. And if so, you've probably spent countless hours compiling a comprehensive set of review questions, only for your students to "break the game" after the first five minutes when they realize that they can just buzz in faster than their opponents with no more than a wild guess.

No thanks.

For this activity, divide students into equal groups (four or five per group is ideal), and have them create a simple matrix like the one shown above with exactly one row and one column for each of a set number of characters or concepts from your current unit of study. Just like a Sudoku puzzle, the goal is for each team to fill in the available squares with items of commonality that only those two items have in common. And since each concept will intersect with another in exactly two different squares inside of the grid, it's a fantastic tool for deeper review. Teams will have to find two unique things that these two concepts have in common in order to complete their matrix.

If you'd like, you can even add a competitive aspect to the activity by setting an overhead timer and seeing which team can complete their grid to the strongest degree before time expires. Prep time: zero minutes. Challenge level: through the roof!

Choose Your Own EDventure Google Forms

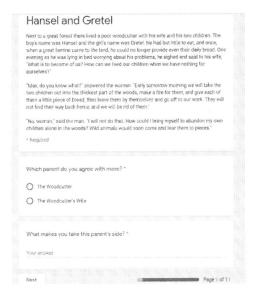

A **Fully Engaged Upgrade to** traditional reading-response journals. You see a fork in the woods. Which path do you choose?

Let's Dig In: Picture this: imagine how much more immersed in a reading assignment your students would be if you could take any bit of textbook content and transform it into a "choose your own adventure"-style quest. And each time students reach a turning point in the tale, they're asked to make a decision to move the adventure along. But before they're allowed to unlock the next chunk of the story, they'll need to explain why they've made the choice that they've made.

Here are three lightning-fast steps to set up this activity for any content you can imagine:

1. Find an online copy of the text you'd like your students to read. Eyeball its length and divide it into X different chunks of relatively equal length. Keep in mind that each chunk will end with a short reflection question (e.g., "What would you do at this point of the adventure?") that lends itself neatly to starting a new page of the form at those junctures where there's a natural break in the action.

2. Create a brand new Google form with X sections and copy/paste the first equal chunk of the story into the text field at the top of the first section. Once a student reaches this page of the form, they'll have the chance to read *only that much* of the story before moving forward to the next installment. See where we're headed?

3. The only way to get to section two of the form is to answer all of the questions at the end of section one (and so on). This is a chance for some serious metacognition! So simply throw a quick "would you rather"-style question at the end of the section to check for student understanding, along with a quick length-validated prompt question where readers will have to explain their rationale for making whatever decision they've made. And since they'll be eager to see where the story goes next, your students will be happy to interact with the text along the way, which makes this an excellent way to get young learners looking for context clues, understanding cause and effect questions, and hitting those ELA standards as they make their way through the unfolding tale of your content.

That's all you'll need for the basic activity! And it's a great way to embed strategic check-for-understanding prompts directly into any piece of assigned reading so that students will need to demonstrate active learning of the material in order to progress through the text.

Google Globetrotters

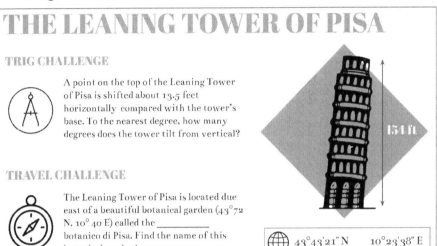

A **Fully Engaged Upgrade to** bringing everyday word problems to life with real-world application. Can you use your wits to survive an amazing race around the globe?

Let's Dig In: This activity transforms any old lesson plan into an action-packed race around the world. Perhaps you're a middle school science class learning about far-flung climates from the North Pole to the Amazon. Or a high school math teacher trying to show your classes the practical applications of complex trigonometry. Whatever you're teaching, this globetrotting spin on traditional word problems is perfect to add life and wonder to any lesson plan—and all you'll need is a stack of printed pages from a Google Slides presentation paired with a handful of coordinates from Google Earth. Ready to race?

Setup is a snap! And the game works like so:

1. Arrange your desks into groups at X locations throughout your room. So as not to create a traffic jam as teams wait for a particular station to become available, you'll want to make sure to have plenty of free stations to choose from. Student teams will "travel" to each of X locations in your classroom, earning stamps on their team's "travel passport" (aka notebook paper or a printed worksheet) whenever they are able to solve a pair of challenges that awaits them at each exotic location. There are two types of problems at each location: a content challenge (word problem related to your course content), and a travel challenge (which can only be solved using the internet).

2. Take whatever word problems might be in your textbook and drop them onto a single page of a slide deck so that each problem gets its own separate slide (like the one shown above). You'll hang these slides around your classroom to help get students up and moving as they make their way around the activity!

3. If you'd like to add visual icons to give each stop along your "fetch quest" an even more game-like feel, head on over to the Noun Project.[4]

4. For the travel challenge, students will need to learn a thing or two about the real-world locale where this particular slide's word problem is set. Maybe they're taking a stroll through the botanical gardens just to the east of the Leaning Tower of Pisa. Or calculating the height of Mount Fuji while braving their way through the tragic secrets of the nearby Aokigahara Forest. You get the idea.

    For the travel challenge, simply pull in a splash of local storytelling or sightseeing from the same neighborhood as the particular item they're looking for from your course content. Perhaps they'll need to use Google Earth to find the name of a particular landmark in the region. Or they'll scan a QR code

---

4 thenounproject.com

taking them to an online encyclopedia where they'll need to discover five facts about a fascinating piece of local folklore before they're allowed to leave the region.

Social Media Smackdown

MLK JR.
@MartinLutherKingJr

Today I said "Hate cannot drive out hate; only love can do that." I hope you all remember to continue the non-violent fight for freedom, justice, and human rights. I hope we'll continue to embrace the ideals and actions from words I've said to inspire #justice #peace #NobelPeacePrize #speech

4:59 PM · Oct 16, 1964 · Twitter for iPhone

DEVELOPING NOW
...RTIN LUTHER KING JR. SHARES SOME INSIGHT ABOUT HIS SPEECH SHARED WITH THE PEOPLE AT THE NOBEL PE...

A Fully Engaged Upgrade to a traditional divide-and-conquer character-recap activity. Can you curate a social media portfolio for the ages?

Let's Dig In: Imagine you and your teammates have just been hired as consultants to a high-powered public relations firm. It's up to you to attract as many eyes to your brand as possible! So each team will need to work with a world-famous client to develop the most well-rounded social media profile in the market today—which means you'll have to help them manage the good, the bad, and the ugly.

- **Create a handful of fake Twitter posts** to help your celebrity client post original tweets to show off their witty personality in 280 characters or less. Use evidence from your course textbook to help inspire you. And don't forget to append relevant hashtags!

- **What sort of images might your client share on Instagram?** Why? Have students post a few photos (or those they can find on the web) that they think would make a great addition to their client's social media portfolio. Drop these items into a Google Slides presentation along with a quick caption or two underneath to help the post feel real!

- **Snapchat stories are for a different audience altogether.** What sort of secrets might your celebrity client be revealing on their Snapchat? And would these stories be public or private?

- **But keep your eye out for clickbait drama!** Even with the savviest PR teams working around the clock, tabloid media is merciless—and celebrity scandals are big business! So what might it look like if TMZ got your celebrity client in their crosshairs?

This activity can easily be scaled to fill anywhere from fifteen to forty-five minutes or longer, so set an overhead timer for as much time as you'd like. Then allow students the chance to work together with their teammates in their respective "spin zones" (small-group desk clusters) as they attempt to curate the strongest and most well-rounded overall social media slide deck on behalf of their client that they can. Will Team Jefferson put together a stronger portfolio than Team Hamilton?

There are countless applications of this activity for subjects ranging from middle school introduction to world languages to advanced level showdowns in high school economics classrooms. The best part is that students of all ages are competing in a playing field where they never quite know how strong their rival's portfolio might be, so they'll want to bring their very best as they get caught up in the excitement of working together to lay the smackdown on their opponent! Just ring the bell and watch your students' creativity shine!

Traps And Treasures

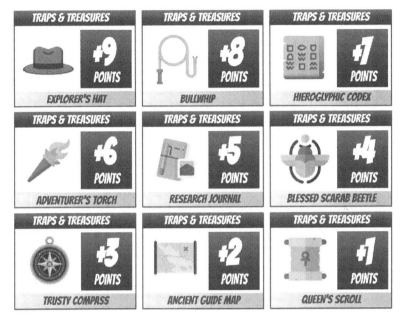

A **Fully Engaged Upgrade to** simple fact-finding or close-reading activities. Pick a mystery envelope and discover the surprises inside!

Let's Dig In: This one is perfect for when you're dividing students into small groups and having them dig through a common text for massive chunks of information. Let's pretend you're teaching poetry to a sixth grade English class and you'd like students to dig into a really long poem to find as many examples of similes, allusions, or metaphors as they can possibly find in a single poem. You've probably done this activity dozens of times: divide students into small teams and assign each group a different item to look for (group one looks for similes, group two for metaphors, etc.). They know the drill!

Now let's add a little salt to punch this traditional staple of small group instruction up and make it feel a bit more game-like. The instructions couldn't be easier: "work with your teammates to find as many examples of thing X, thing Y or thing Z as you can before time expires. Write down your answers on a sheet of paper for your team. You'll score one point for each thing you can find. And the team with the most points when time expires wins. The end."

No really, that's it. It's that simple.

The only twist?

Before the activity starts, you've already reviewed the poem that teams will be scanning with an eye toward whichever X, Y, or Z elements you'd like each group to look for. And you already know before the activity begins that certain items will be *much* easier to find than other ones. So you decide to add an element of surprise into this otherwise ho-hum close-reading activity by letting each group select a mystery envelope to determine what all their team will be looking for. That way, the playing field is leveled and nobody knows for sure which item they'll be looking for before the "game" begins.

And here's the best part:

Since you know in advance that some items are easier to find than others, you hide a series of "traps and treasures" inside each of these envelopes to help even up the odds. If you want to help sweeten the deal for a particularly challenging look-for item, perhaps you'll have thrown a hidden bonus point value (+5 extra points, for example) into one envelope to help give that team a booster rocket to start their search with a chunk of freebie points to build their confidence. Or if you're feeling really sneaky, you can even throw in a few envelopes with a "trap" that starts teams off at a slight disadvantage (like beginning the challenge with ˜3 points).

But it's only when that countdown timer begins that teams are allowed to do the big reveal and see whether they've taken home a station packed with treasures or loaded with traps. Some stations will contain bonus point "treasures" that give students an endowed-progress sense of beginner's luck, starting them off with a few freebie points and encouraging them to work harder so as not to lose their early lead. Other stations, meanwhile contain "traps" (which deduct the total amount of points a team will begin the activity to start with). And guess what?

When a group starts their showdown already in the hole, the teacher can remind them that surely only the *easiest* stations would ever come with an early disadvantage—meaning those students will immediately begin working *that much harder* since your cleverly placed trap will have convinced them that they are surely the odds-on-favorite to come out the winner by the time the final bell sounds.

Hexagonal Thinking

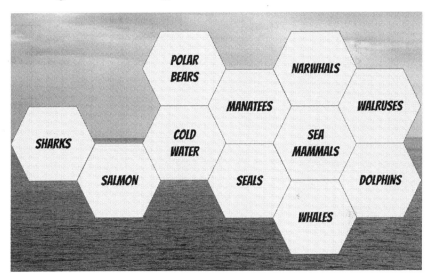

 A Fully Engaged Upgrade to mind-mapping or cause-and-effect activities.

Let's Dig In: This little technique might seem overwhelming at the start. But hang in there. This is a gem of a gem. So let's get you up to speed so you can start rolling with hexagonal thinking. It all begins with the humble hexagon!

This little guy finds its way into many board games for its versatility. It's often used to create modular boards that change from game to game as you can lay the tiles out in a myriad of ways. This is exactly what happens with hexagonal thinking. Students are challenged to create giant hexagonally tiled boards of interconnected content. This is a great review activity when you are well into a unit. Begin by creating a list of concepts, vocab terms—even images!—and other important details from your current unit. Then place those details on bunches and bunches of hexagons. Print those suckers out and stash a set in a different envelope for each team. And just like that: you're ready to play!

Now we get to see that constructivist classroom in action. Give teams of three to five students an envelope filled with your chosen concepts and a giant piece of paper to put them on. Students then pour out the envelope and start to sift through all the concepts. Each hex has six sides with which they can create connections.

Their mission? Use as many of the hexes as possible in the time they're given. Students place each new hexagon next to previously placed ones, all the while making sure they're prepared to defend each of the unique sides along which the hexagon connects to its neighbors (how is X like Y? How is X like Z?). Once you begin, you start to see the magic of this lesson. Students erupt in conversations about the content. Which connections should we make? How can we lay out all of these connections in as logical a fashion as we can without painting ourselves into a corner? Before your eyes, students start to think of groups of words that work together like a giant "honeycomb"—but then must connect each group back to the whole.

This is a guaranteed hit for all parties involved. Your students will love the freedom to play with the content, and you will be proud to hear the conversations happening all around your classroom.

Inventor Sprint

A Fully Engaged Upgrade to loosening the dreaded writer's block.

Let's Dig In: Human beings love to create, but sometimes it's really hard to get started. Other times, it's hard to think of something new. That's where the idea of Inventor Sprints and Workshop Whirlwinds can be a total game-changer. Sometimes all we need is a bit of a push or a catalyst to create a spark that can set our imaginations on fire. And playing with the precious scarcity of time is one of the game mechanics that can help us do just that.

Here is where the joy of under-the-gun innovation can really come into play. Both the Inventor Sprint and the Workshop Whirlwind activities use time to help get us into that elusive state of flow. We've used them as ungraded exercises in our classrooms, our Twitter communities, and even in our PD events to get ideas flowing. They have all resulted in an explosion of innovation!

First: the Inventor Sprint. Give your group about five minutes to create a response to a visual prompt. For example: take a look at the castle image above, and try to invent some sort of mythical item, enchanted hero's badge, or short-story vignette based solely off of the picture. Five minutes on the clock. On your mark, get set, GO!

Add an extra layer of life to the game by splitting your students into smaller teams and giving them the same amount of time to flesh out their creation before bringing it back to share with the combined group. This is exhilarating and exhausting at the same time! This is a lightning-fast, zero-prep activity that can inspire countless adventures related to your course content. So lean into the experience and really test yourself!

Workshop Whirlwind

A **Fully Engaged Upgrade** to lethargy and good old-fashioned laziness (we've all been there).

Let's Dig In: Let's play with the eustress of that ticking clock one more time with the Workshop Whirlwind. This one uses the time mechanic again. For this activity, you'll probably want to give each group about 10 minutes to put their thoughts together. In the Workshop Whirlwind, your goal is to ask a single "what if" question about a common prompt and see how many solutions the members of your group can dream up before time expires. Their goal? Add as many ideas as they can to answer whatever this prompt might be asking!

Research shows that it can be especially challenging to have our creative brain and our analytical brain working to their peak efficiency at the same exact time. But this activity is a no-stress, no-prep way to help your students kickstart a bunch of clever, creative ideas before getting to all the harder stuff of narrowing down their choices. First we brain dump, then we workshop: both in a low stakes environment.

When everyone in the room is in agreement that we're still in a very early stage of the drafting process together, there's zero pressure to make "the perfect thing" out of thin air all at once. This takes the sting out of coming up with ideas. Of course some ideas might end up being more feasible or fruitful than others, and that's precisely the point! Simply set a timer for a creative brain dump where even the wildest suggestions are welcome and encouraged. And when time is up, give students the chance to scour back through the newly created pile of ideas to size up which among them seem most viable and exciting.

Think about how powerful this activity could be for helping a classroom full of students dream up possible ideas for research papers, technological innovations, or good old-fashioned essay topics!

We've run this activity with fellow educators on Twitter and, in one thirty-minute-long chat, we had over forty ideas created that were all usable for any classroom. This is the power of the Workshop Whirlwind! Not only does it test your creative stamina, but it leaves you empowered with the knowledge that one can create in a time crunch.

Questions for Discussion

Your first challenge is to make a choice! Here we've given you some great places to begin your journey toward a fully engaged classroom. These lesson activities can work in just about any classroom. Take a moment and go back and reread one or two of these ideas. Now ask yourself which one you are committed to doing in the next two weeks. What would your first prep-steps be?

We've all heard that voice and choice play an important role in making students feel empowered by their learning. So let's take a look at our own classrooms: how much choice do we really provide? Break it down on three levels.

- First, look at the semester and ask yourself: How much choice do I anticipate my students will get within this half of the year?
- Then bring it into clearer focus by asking yourself about the next month.
- After that, look at the next week. What small steps can you take to introduce more opportunities for choice in the next seven days of instruction?

What fears do you have about offering your students more open-ended experiences in your classroom? How can we empower our students to own *their* critical thinking and creative expression without putting them on *our* rails of rules and rubrics? Taking that list of fears, what are ones that you are in control of? How might you support yourself so that you can get out of students' way? How can we offer students more challenging, open-ended tasks in order to create opportunities for them to explore and chart their own success?

CHAPTER FOUR

IMAGINATION AND ITERATION

Cogito, ergo sum:
"I think, therefore I am."

—René Descartes

Hi again! John here. I remember how, when I was a kid, every few months my parents used to take me or one of my two brothers to a small, private medical practice called the Somerset Pediatric Group, located about twenty minutes or so from our family's home in a tiny sub-suburban farm-country town in northwestern New Jersey. My guess is that our friendly neighborhood doctor's office probably looked pretty similar to the one near you.

Long before the world ever had a term for "social distancing," my parents rested easy knowing that the Pediatric Group had a special "sick kids" entrance in the back so families with children who might be running a fever could steer clear of patients who were just dropping in for routine checkups in the front lobby. And for most visits, a trip to the doctor's office typically meant little more than a half hour of sitting around a well-lit waiting area, a quick checkup in one of those two or three small exam rooms (complete with padded tables and those big standing metal scales to check your height and weight!), and a friendly "thank you" send-off at the front desk when you were done, where you'd get a sticker or a lollipop for being so brave. The place was friendly and welcoming, running like a well-oiled machine with a regular rotating cast of three incredibly warm, intelligent, and talented physicians—each one kinder and more compassionate than the last to help us get through the hard stuff when duty called.

For your average card-carrying member of the under-twelve-crowd, it was a pretty sweet deal.

Yet, without fail, on one out of every three trips to the doctor's office, like clockwork, my poor parents would have to deal with the fact that one of their kids would inevitably freak out and have a total meltdown from the moment we saw which of the three pediatricians happened to be in the building that day. Remarkably, our irrational behavior had nothing to do with whether or not we were there for a regularly scheduled checkup or in for a visit on a day home from school with a fever. Instead, it was the mere mention of the on-call doctor's name alone that was enough to send us into hysterics.

The doctors' names?

Michael Fragoso.

Eric Yorke.

And, I kid you not . . .

Jack Needleman.

Now, sure, there was always the occasional booster shot or vaccine to be administered regardless of which doctor was working on a given day. But I'll give you two guesses as to which of these three men's names made our fight-or-flight reactions kick into overdrive from the moment we stepped foot inside that door. Put yourself inside the mind of an overanxious six-year-old for a moment and see if you can follow our logic:

"Superman" was faster than a locomotive and could leap tall buildings in a single bound.

"Spider-Man" could climb walls and shoot webs out of his hands.

But "Needleman"!?!

We laugh. Surely this is just a kid's overactive imagination all too prone to the power of suggestion, right? ("It hurts more because I think it's going to hurt"). And, true, without fail, the actual pinprick of each rare injection was far less traumatic than all the dread and anxiety we'd build up on our way into that exam room. Yet this simple story of a child's innocent misconception can actually help us pull back the curtain to take a much broader and more complex look at the fascinatingly limitless potential of the human mind.

Absent a story, we tend to invent one using whatever scraps of imaginings we happen to have available to us at a given time. As teachers, perhaps we can learn how to harness a child's overactive imagination in our classrooms and put these natural storytelling tendencies to good use.

APPAREL OFT PROCLAIMS THE MAN

Sometimes, changing the way someone sees their situation can come from something as trivial as a new item of clothing. Call it a Dumbo feather or a grown-up spin on childhood dress-up. But the science behind it checks out. It's the reason why we feel more tranquil hanging around the house in Yoga pants. Why we feel a little bit faster when we slip on a pair of running shorts. Or why you start to hear the imaginary fanfare in your ears every time you take a swig of your favorite sports drink and lace up your sneakers "Like Mike."

If you've ever felt like a boss simply by suiting up in the right clothes for the job, you're certainly not alone. Scientists call this phenomenon *enclothed cognition*—and research suggests there's a clear connection between how we dress and how we start to see ourselves when taking on specifically challenging tasks. Take, for example, a 2019 study from a team of researchers based out of North Carolina State University in Raleigh, North Carolina. In this study, two groups of fifth grade students were randomly assigned to one of two groups for a slate of ten science classes taught by their classroom science teacher. Half of the students were placed into a treatment group that wore lab coats, while the other half served as the control group that did not wear lab coats. Shakespeare himself couldn't have scripted a more poetic outcome:

> Results showed students' interest in science was not significantly changed due to wearing the lab coat, *but the lab coats did have significant effects on students' perceived recognition by others as being a science learner* (emphasis added). Furthermore, those treatment students with low self-efficacy (compared to those with high self-efficacy) and those with who did not report having access to a parent with a STEM career had significant increases in perceptions of self-efficacy in science.[1]

As a classroom teacher, it's certainly something to keep in mind as we go forward. Could something as small as putting on a lab coat make us feel more like a scientist? Could interviewing people for a story in the school newspaper while wearing a simple lanyard with the words "Press Credentials" actually make a student a better writer? And could using a flashlight to look at a worksheet about ancient cave paintings that's taped to the underside of a table somehow change the way our students start to envision themselves as self-styled "experts" in a content area?

A ROSE BY ANY OTHER NAME

There's a fascinating offshoot to the field of enclothed cognition that *New Scientist* calls "nominative determinism"—which basically states that our names can dramatically affect the people that we become. And once we start to call ourselves a certain name, then we start to act a certain way. It's like Carol Dweck's fixed mindset with the volume turned up to eleven: we hear ourselves called a thing so much that we actually

---

1   M. Gail Jones, Tammy Lee, Katherine Chesnutt, et al., "Enclothed Cognition: Putting Lab Coats to the Test," *International Journal of Science Education* 41, no. 14 (August 2019): 1962–1976, doi.org/10.1080/09500693.2019.1649504.

start to believe it. Winners win. Losers lose, right? And if you're born into a name like "Victor" or "Victoria," you might actually go through life believing that success is your birthright.

Is it any coincidence that the fastest man on the planet just so happens to have been born with the last name "Bolt?"

Don't laugh: a 2002 study published in the *Journal of Personality and Social Psychology* by Brett Pelham, a psychology professor at Montgomery College in Maryland, and colleagues Matthew Mirenberg and John Jones found that people named "Dennis" or "Denise" tend to become dentists at a higher rate than people of other equally popular names. And a 2013 study from Pelham and Mauricio Carvallo, a psychology professor at the University of Oklahoma, suggests that men were 15.5 percent more likely to work in occupations that bore their surname than they should have been when compared to cases based on a simple random distribution by chance.[2]

Paging Dr. Needleman, right?

THE POWER OF A NAME AND THE LEGEND OF THE 6-2'S

Whether it's in the way you dress or the titles by which you are addressed by those around you, the more frequently a person hears or sees themselves as a "born talent" or an "expert" in their field, the more their imagination kicks in to try and start making these dreams a reality. So what might happen if we changed the way we refer to the "students" in our classroom?

In *As You Like It,* William Shakespeare famously wrote:

> All the world's a stage,
> And all the men and women merely players;
> They have their exits and their entrances,
> And one man in his time plays many parts.

---

2 S. J. Velasquez, "Do Our Names Push Us towards Certain Jobs?," BBC Worklife, April 4, 2018, bbc.com/worklife/article/20180404-do-our-names-push-us-toward-certain-jobs.

Three centuries later in *The Crucible*, American playwright Arthur Miller echoed this same idea of a heroic character offering a powerful meditation on the many roles one plays in life. Near the end of the play, John Proctor, who was sentenced to be hanged, gives an impassioned speech. The court asked him to sign his name to a binding legal document that would state he was guilty of the charges before him, which he wasn't. Proctor refuses to sign the document even though it would have spared his life. Though he was willing to lie and fake a confession out loud, he refuses to sign his name to the paper saying as much. His reason, he shouts, "Because it is my name! Because I cannot have another in my life."

This is a powerful statement. Think about your own name. What crosses your mind when you say it? What crosses the mind of others when they hear it? What part do you play? Like it or not, there is a whole lot "in" a name.

This idea of a name and its importance still resonates. And so many things in our classrooms are set up for the business of school and not for the inherent humanity of the students themselves. Block one. Period four. Third quarter. It's all just so . . . mechanical.

In most schools each class is given a number—not a name, but a number. Ask yourself, if you were an eleven- or twelve-year-old child, would you remember that you were in "section 6-2?" Would you even care? This is a clear example of a system that was set up to prioritize the efficiency of the school and not the humanity of the student. While this is understandable, it is our job to be the best for our students.

"6-2."

What does that mean to you?

What feelings do you have when you hear it? Most people will fall into one of two camps. First, and most likely, it feels cold and soulless. At best, if you're part of the second group, you think in numbers, spreadsheets, and algorithms all day. But if so, then all you hear is another number, an organizational technique with data to file away with countless other lines of sorting systems and binary code.

No matter what group you're in, it's clear that the name 6-2 wasn't given to inspire students or make them feel a part of something. The name 6-2 has been just a placeholder to organize the schedule. Imagine you brought home a brand new puppy: Would you ever even think to give it a name like "6-2"? Of course not! This is precisely the sort of stale holdover element from the "old" Game of School that is ripe for some much-needed imagination and iteration.

Names matter. They convey a sense of belonging. An aura of importance. A fresh identity that elevates them above the white background noise of yesteryear. So why not do the same thing with the names of each of your class sections? In a gamified classroom, we can transport students into any far-off worlds that we can imagine. We can be scientific explorers bravely venturing to the deepest depths of the ocean. We can be aspiring rock stars setting out to craft the perfect set list for a sold-out nationwide tour. We can even invent brand new realms that invite students to venture into fantastical worlds of myth, legend, and magic. This allows teachers to ditch the stodgy "6-2" nomenclature to transform each class section into a legendary land of medieval houses. "6-2" becomes the House of Remal, "6-5" is the powerful House of Torin, "6-6" is the mighty House of Zemar, and lastly "6-8" turns into the House of Aleria.

It might sound simple, or even too easy. But students now feel a part of something larger than themselves. They belong to something. At the start of the year, they have been handed the torch of their house. It is in their hands whether their house will succeed or fail. Those who have come before have left their legacy, but it is the current students who decide the house's future. Now, when an eleven-year-old hears that, they get excited and proud of their newfound place in the history of 6-2 . . . or rather, the House of Remal!

This is just one example of the power in a name. Names can transform how we feel about ourselves, the activities we take part in, and the outcomes we produce. Think about the theme of your class. Challenge yourself to create an experience for your students. Think about what you call things in your classroom, from tests and quizzes to courses and content. What might be re-imagined?

American automotive industry pioneer Henry Ford famously quipped: "Whether you think you can or you think you can't, you're right." Imagination inspires iteration. And if our classrooms can make a consistent, concerted effort to creating immersive worlds of playful learning where our students imagine themselves as experts in the field, there's no limit to what they can achieve.

BLOOM'S WHERE YOU'RE PLANTED

Let's face it: A child's imagination is a powerful, powerful thing. But with rote memorization drills, one-size-fits all homework, and countless hours spent cramming for standardized exams, traditional school rarely gives students the opportunity to flex their imaginative muscles. Which feels like a ton of missed opportunities, given what we know from the basics of Bloom's taxonomy. In short, imagination requires tremendous cognitive ability and demands some of the highest levels of learning! Ever notice that it's much easier to turn on a familiar TV show late at night than it is to devote the brain power required to reading a novel?

A quick refresher in Bloom's taxonomy to make sure we're all starting on the same page:

In 2001, a group of cognitive psychologists, curriculum theorists, and instructional researchers published *A Taxonomy for Teaching, Learning, and Assessment*—a contemporary reworking of the original model put forth by American educational psychologist Benjamin Bloom, which had long been celebrated as a cornerstone of effective classroom teaching practice. Let's take a quick look at the tasks and verbs that the team put forth for each of the six "levels" of the new learning pyramid, and make note at which of these stages you begin seeing words related to imagination come into play:

Remember	<ul><li>recognizing (identifying)</li><li>recalling (retrieving)</li></ul>
Understand	<ul><li>interpreting (clarifying, paraphrasing, representing, translating)</li><li>exemplifying (illustrating, instantiating)</li><li>classifying (categorizing, subsuming)</li><li>summarizing (abstracting, generalizing)</li><li>inferring (concluding, extrapolating, interpolating, predicting)</li><li>comparing (contrasting, mapping, matching)</li><li>explaining (constructing models)</li></ul>
Apply	<ul><li>executing (carrying out)</li><li>implementing (using)</li></ul>
Analyze	<ul><li>differentiating (discriminating, distinguishing, focusing, selecting)</li><li>organizing (finding coherence, integrating, outlining, parsing, structuring)</li><li>attributing (deconstructing)</li></ul>
Evaluate	<ul><li>checking (coordinating, detecting, monitoring, testing)</li><li>critiquing (judging)</li></ul>
Create	<ul><li>generating (hypothesizing)</li><li>planning (designing)</li><li>producing (construct)[3]</li></ul>

Did you notice a pattern? The highest levels of learning demand the deepest levels of thinking. And it's no coincidence that it's at these same highest levels of thinking where we start to see all the words like "detecting," "judging," "designing," and "constructing." These words are most closely related to imagination itself. Whether we're playing dress up or calling ourselves aspirational names inspired by our specific field of study, imaginative learning and complex thinking go hand in hand. So why aren't we spending more of our instructional time tapping into the power of play in our everyday instruction?

---

3 Lorin W. Anderson, David R. Krathwohl, and Benjamin S. Bloom, *A Taxonomy for Learning, Teaching, and Assessing : A Revision of Bloom's Taxonomy of Educational Objectives*, Lorin W. Anderson and David Krathwohl, eds., with contributors Peter W. Airasian, et al. (New York: Longman, 2001).

TIME TO PLAY THE GAME

In the pages that follow, we've provided an array of imaginative activity templates and the ground rules for each of these game-like teaching techniques. Some of them are new iterations of activities that we've reimagined with even more excitement since the publication of *eXPlore Like a Pirate* and *EDrenaline Rush*, while others are brand new! We are proud to share them with you in our never-ending commitment to creating classrooms where students are fully engaged. But please, don't be afraid to put your own twist on any of the resources you see here and tailor them to the unique needs of your learners. Imagination and iteration go hand in hand! And as anyone who's ever plunged into a living room floor made of molten hot lava could tell you—"house rules" can often be some of the best parts of any game.

> Ray Kroc is widely credited with helping turn a tiny California hamburger chain owned by the McDonald brothers into the world's largest global restaurant franchise. The scope of his lifelong commitment to imagination and iteration can perhaps best be summed up by this quote-worthy phrase: "Are you green and growing, or ripe and rotting?"
>
> Iteration in instructional design means making a similar commitment to studying not just what works, but how it can continue to improve. And to help the ideas in this book have limitless room for growth long after the final page has ended, we've built an entire website where teachers from all around the world join together to share student engagement strategies, activities, lesson ideas, and professional development resources to help change the Game of School.
>
> If you'd like to join this passionate community of imaginative educators, visit EMC2Learning.com.

CLASS IS LAVA!

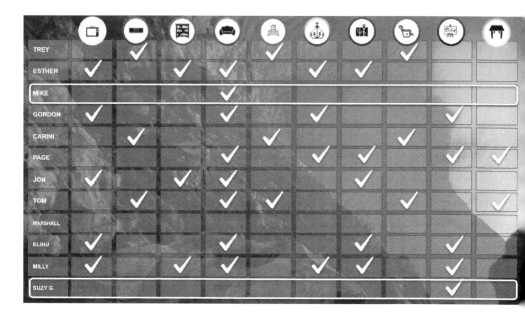

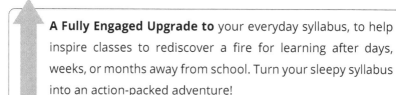

Imagine a World Where: Our favorite childhood game of hopping on the furniture could inspire students to hotfoot their way back into your classroom!

A Fully Engaged Upgrade to your everyday syllabus, to help inspire classes to rediscover a fire for learning after days, weeks, or months away from school. Turn your sleepy syllabus into an action-packed adventure!

On the heels of the COVID-19 pandemic, thousands of schools around the country shifted their instruction to classes that were entirely online. That "new normal" gave way to a world where asynchronous "on-demand" learning became the law of the land, and both teachers and students needed to familiarize themselves with a boatload of new digital teaching strategies lest they found themselves sinking like a stone! So why not steal a "binge-worthy" teaching approach from the king of streaming services as you introduce students to a bunch of new classroom protocols?

Enter the Class is Lava.

In the hit Netflix show *Floor is Lava*, contestants need to use their wits and hop across half-submerged furniture as they make their way across a room that's rapidly filling with molten orange goo. So will you jump on the table, then dive onto the recliner? Or climb the curtains before swinging to the sofa? The choice is totally up to you and there are all sorts of paths one can take to make their way across any given room, but the one rule is simply not to lose your footing because "the floor is lava!"

Now picture this: a similarly themed classroom challenge where students work independently or in competing teams to complete ten different activities before the final bell rings. Before you know it, your classroom (in person or on the video call) is a-flurry with teams of students buzzing around in every direction as they:

- Sign up for text alerts using the messaging platform Remind.
- Complete an "about me" survey using a Google form.
- Screen a short clip on YouTube about some unique advantages of remote learning.
- Take a photo of something that represents them and share it in a virtual show and tell.
- Submit a short writing sample and practice turning it in using your school's LMS.
- Complete a personality quiz to provide a few thoughts about how they learn best.
- Watch an Edpuzzle where they meet the teacher and answer a few quick questions.
- Film a short video where they pronounce their name and share their pronouns.
- Meet as a small group in a Zoom breakout room to share their learning goals for the year.

- Take a five-question Quizizz and learn the basics of how to complete nightly homework.

Instead of hopping on actual pieces of furniture, students are virtually "hopping" between a series of quick to-do items like completing a short Flipgrid video or filling out a Google form. A team is permitted to navigate these challenges one at a time, in any order they'd like. And when they stick the landing at a particular station? Nice work! Have them call you in (on Zoom or in the room) to cross it off of their checklist and make their way toward another activity of their choice. But if a group calls you over to check out their progress at a particular station and the work has fallen short of the mark? Those students will have to spend a few minutes "rescuing one another from the lava" while stuck at that station without being permitted to move onto their next task until everything is sorted out properly. (All the while watching rival teams move *that much further* along up the scoreboard!)

The obstacles for each classroom will inevitably change to suit the unique needs of the day's lesson plan. But adding even an early layer of choice, imagination, and autonomy to what quickly becomes a self-guided path toward success helps every student feel safe and supported as they learn that taking appropriate academic risks can become increasingly rewarding.

Twenty-first century learning is not without its share of pitfalls. And while we're not quite hopping onto entertainment centers or chandeliers in order to avoid being swallowed by colorful sludge, "hopping" onto all sorts of resources to help us keep our classrooms afloat is a total lifesaver!

PARDON THE INTERRUPTION

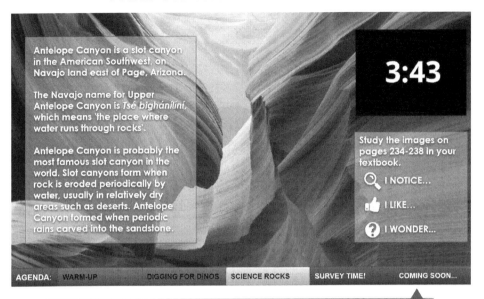

Antelope Canyon is a slot canyon in the American Southwest, on Navajo land east of Page, Arizona.

The Navajo name for Upper Antelope Canyon is *Tsé bighánílíní*, which means 'the place where water runs through rocks'.

Antelope Canyon is probably the most famous slot canyon in the world. Slot canyons form when rock is eroded periodically by water, usually in relatively dry areas such as deserts. Antelope Canyon formed when periodic rains carved into the sandstone.

3:43

Study the images on pages 234-238 in your textbook.

I NOTICE...

I LIKE...

I WONDER...

AGENDA: WARM-UP   DIGGING FOR DINOS   SCIENCE ROCKS   SURVEY TIME!   COMING SOON...

Imagine a World Where: The daily to-do list of your lesson plan is presented in the fast-paced, slick, and super-engaging style of television programming made famous by "the world-wide leader in sports." Let's face it: our students spend hours outside of the classroom hanging on every bit of news from their favorite players and athletic teams. So why not present your lesson plan like you were inside a living episode of primetime sports coverage à la ESPN? All you'll need to do is insert a handful of brightly colored rectangles at the bottom of your slide deck!

A Fully Engaged Upgrade to giving your slide presentations some breathing room!

This is especially helpful for maintaining student interest over longer class periods, particularly in physical classrooms (or online classes!) that depend on multistep lesson plans or a time-bound sequence of daily routines. See that handy little ticker bar along the bottom of the image just above the previous paragraph? Quickly add life and structure to a single class period of any length with the simple addition of a "ticker" ribbon at the bottom of your presentation slides. It's just a series of small rectangles, created in Google Slides and nestled quietly away at the bottom of the presentation. Your students will have a clear sense of endowed progress as they make their way through the lesson without your running agenda commandeering a massive chunk of your presentation screen. Pretty cool, right?

In an individual slide, embedding a countdown timer lets students know not to panic because a clear end is always in sight. Along the bottom menu, completed agenda items can be grayed out one activity at a time as you go, giving students a mounting sense of accomplishment as the class unfolds. This also provides a sneak peek of challenges that still loom over the horizon (and it's a great place to leave prescheduled breaks for the restroom, questions, etc.).

TWO TEAMS AND A TURNCOAT

Imagine a World Where: Students are honing their communication skills and social deduction strategies to see if they can identify a secret "mole" in their midst!

A Fully Engaged Upgrade to teaching methods of persuasion, lessons on peer-to-peer communication, and any course content about traitors, treasons, and about-faces.

One of the best things about most tabletop games is that they are really little more than a handful of printed cards with a few player tokens. This makes them prime subjects for iteration! Certain party games might be tons of fun, but they simply aren't quite school appropriate.

Let's take a look at how a problematic off-the-shelf product can become an absolute blast in the classroom.

Two Rooms and a Boom is a social deduction game (think Heads Up, Seven Up, but with explosions! Or Mafia with less time spent watching from the sidelines). Once you pass out the cards, groups of anywhere from ten to thirty players are instantly transported into a massive game of "do you know that I know that you know?"—which is whole bunch of fun. The only problem? The default game is themed with a pretty non-school-appropriate story line. Here's the official game description:

> Stop your President from being blown up! But who is the President? More importantly . . . Who is the Bomber?! In this social game of hidden roles and deduction, players are divided into 2 different rooms. Find your teammates, establish trust, and exchange hostages before time runs out and the bomb explodes! It's the party game that's always a blast.

Yeah. Suicide bombers and countdown timers to secret explosions? Not exactly the sort of thing we'd feel comfortable rolling out with a room full of students. But what if you kept the same "guess who's on your team" activity and nixed the whole "blow up the president" angle, instead using the default game rules to create a more school-friendly team-vs-team scenario?

Say hello to Two Teams and a Turncoat!

Just like its off-the-shelf counterpart, this activity is a game of secret identities, and each student will be given a color-coded card with their specific allegiance on it. In this game, knowledge is power! And whatever information (and how much of it and with whom) each player chooses to share from their card is completely up to each individual student. If you're on the blue team, you're an American colonist, and your goal is to get George Washington out of the "room" and away from the traitorous Benedict Arnold. Meanwhile, if you're on the red team, you're a British redcoat. Your goal is to get George Washington into the same room as that notorious turncoat.

The only catch? Nobody knows who's who—or who they can trust—when the game begins! Over the course of a series of timed rounds, players will work individually and as teams to forge delicate alliances as they share information from their own cards with any other players. No joke: your students will go absolutely wild for this one!

Head to the Two Rooms and a Boom website for the complete rulebook for this game (available for free!).[4] Here's a lightning-fast four-step makeover on how to turn this nowhere-near-school-appropriate game into an immediate blast for your classroom:

1. Grab a stack of index cards and mark twelve of them as "Patriots" using a blue marker (for the colonists) and twelve of them as "Redcoats" using a red marker (for the British).
2. Throw in some clever double-crossing by creating a pair of undercover spies for each side. To do so, simply create two British spy cards by writing the word "Redcoat" in blue ink,

4 tuesdayknightgames.com/tworoomsandaboom

and create two additional colonist spy cards by writing the word "Patriot" in red ink. Sneaky, eh?

3. Mark exactly one additional blue card "George Washington" (the head honcho of the Americans), and exactly one additional red card with the word "Turncoat" (the notorious Benedict Arnold himself!).

You're now ready to play.

Suddenly your classes are competing to save the thirteen colonies while imagining themselves as soldiers on either side of the American Revolution. Will you be able to catch the notorious Benedict Arnold? Same gameplay as the original, but WAY more appropriate for a school-based setting.

Or in a world language classroom: "Two Rooms et Tu Brute?!" With virtually zero advance prep required, you're teaching course content while students are practicing speaking in the target language in real time! The possibilities are really as wide open as your imagination.

Iteration to the rescue! Note that whatever remix you put on the activity, it is at its core *the exact same game as before*. All you needed to do was give the original product a new, school-appropriate coat of paint by writing a bunch of color-coded words on a stack of index cards.

FANTASY FOOTBALL DRAFT

Imagine a World Where: Student teams compete to assemble the strongest overall roster to fit the unique requirements of your curriculum. Maybe they're gathering the most treacherous characters in all of Shakespeare? Compiling wish lists of the most vital elements required to sustain life on an uncharted planet? Or putting together a dream team of the bravest historical leaders the world has ever seen? You're on the clock—let the games begin!

A Fully Engaged Upgrade to independent or small team-based research and fact-finding.

With minimal prep, a little imagination can help students inject all sorts of life and energy into otherwise sleepy independent research or annotated bibliography type assignments. Using the familiar concept of an NFL-style player draft, teams compete against rival squads as coaches of their respective franchise, racing against the clock while vying to showcase which "dream team" has what it takes to dominate the field of play.

Let's pretend you're in a fifth grade science classroom that's studying a unit about major milestones in technology. Here's the activity setup:

1. Before class begins, divide students into teams of four to five members each.

2. Queue up some epic NFL-style music as your students enter the classroom with a quick countdown timer announcing that

the "Inaugural Inventor's Draft" is about to begin in just a few short moments.

3. Greet your students with an expectant smile as they make their way to their desk groups.

4. Then hit them with the big reveal: "Welcome to the Inaugural Inventors Draft! Your goal is to work with your teammates to draft a team that will leave the competition in the dust! Each team will have the chance to build their dream roster of the five most influential inventors of the twentieth century. You are allowed to select anyone you'd like! And each team will be on the clock drafting at the same time, so it's OK if you draft the same player as a rival squad. But you'll need to be prepared to defend your selections! Use the editable text on the slide template to back up your claims!"

Set an overhead timer for as long as you'd like, then sit back and see what your students can do as the draft is officially underway. Feel free to fire up some exciting sports music in the background and make your way between groups to check in on their progress and ask clarifying questions to each team as they go. You are the league's commissioner, after all!

Students can use the web or any in-class resources (textbooks, specific examples from novels read in class, etc.) to bolster their findings—highlighting each draftee's attributes by providing relevant hyperlinks to credible sources and text evidence as they go.

When time expires, it's on to the presentation round, where teams defend their choices, and then on to the post-draft analysis, where rival teams have the chance to become ESPN-like "talking heads." Here, students pinpoint the strengths and weaknesses of each of the opposing squads.

And in the end, the commissioner of the league makes a judgment call on which squad has done the best job in each phase of the game (the draft, the presentation, and the post-draft analysis). Or better yet, give the power to the people and let the "players' union" (aka your students) vote on which team has fared the best. Playful iteration at its finest!

VIRTUAL BIKE RIDE

Imagine a World Where: You've hopped on one of those fancy new "smart bicycles" (like Peloton or SoulCycle) and with a push of a button, you set your destination to any place you can imagine, and you're taking a virtual bike ride anywhere in the known world (or beyond it)!

A Fully Engaged Upgrade to activities where students need to research a particular location or environment. Exploring the molten hot cores of cone volcanoes or the best-kept secrets of Parisian tourist hotspots? Why not let your students take center stage and become the stars of your virtual world tour? It's *Flat Stanley* for the twenty-first century!

Picture this: you're a third grade science classroom learning all about the Mesozoic era. How much fun would it be to take a virtual class trip through the Triassic, Jurassic, and Cretaceous periods? Ms. Frizzle would be proud!

Or let's flip the script and pretend that you're an AP Spanish class learning about the legends of Chichén Itzá. Take a step back in time and explore ancient Mayan ruins in Mexico!

Here's the setup:

1. Divide your class into teams of three to five students apiece.
2. Ask these groups to imagine they are rival high-tech computer rendering companies, each of which is vying to be hired by a cutting-edge exercise company (like Peloton or SoulCycle). Their task: create a virtual workout that will take cyclists on a 360° tour of the content that your course is currently studying.
3. Remind these rival teams to keep in mind that your clients pay top dollar for your virtual spin classes! And let them know that the folks who subscribe to your monthly online membership are fanatical about their high expectations and their attention to detail in the virtual bike rides that they take. Your exercise company is the industry leader for a reason, so money is no object!
4. Now sit back and let your students put the pedal to the metal!

Let your young explorers track down the perfect images and landmarks to flesh out each leg of these imaginary journeys, with all the right details as they put those fun Easter eggs and personal twists on their virtual showcases. What other riders might live in the world of their themed adventure? What songs would make the perfect soundtrack for a workout playlist inspired by what you're studying? And how excited would students be to come to school the following day to share these creations with their classmates?

IMAGE BATTLE ROYALE

Imagine a World Where: Students compete to find pictures on the web that best represent a particular concept you're studying in class. But only one submission will take home the crown!

A Fully Engaged Upgrade to any old day. This lesson enhancer is one that can be peppered into just about any day. Find yourself with a little extra time? Do this! Need a pop of excitement? Do this! The Image Battle Royale is an activity that helps build collaborative skills with groups while also pushing students to think outside the box.

The setup is easy. Create one Google Slide presentation for your room. Depending on the number of students you have, you might want to have it be a two-slide show. Divide each of the slides into four quadrants. Make sure that each quadrant has a group number or name. Set the editing permissions of the slides to anyone with the link.

> **PRO TIP:** Make the slides ahead of time, export them as images, then set an image as the background and delete all the text and quadrant graphics. That way students won't accidentally change the layout of the quadrants or delete the team names.

Now share the link with the students and give them a short amount of time to find an image that they believe best represents a fitting visual for the given prompt. Remind them that in this game, thinking literally isn't required—in fact, it could end up hurting you in the long run—and they will be given fifteen to thirty seconds to explain their images at the end of the round. Points will be awarded based on creativity and uniqueness. For example, let's say the vocabulary term was *Nile River*. Half a dozen different photos of the same body of water probably won't win your team any points for creativity!

Inspired to think outside the box, groups intuitively begin to explore beyond literal images with one-to-one connections, and they use their fifteen-second explanations at the end of the round to share what they've discovered. Perhaps one student posts a simple picture of a wrapped gift and offers the explanation that the Nile was a gift to the Egyptians. This short yet elegant answer is the kind of thing that can blow us away!

In addition to being unique and creative, these out-of-the-box creations are quick ways for students to demonstrate knowledge of the course material with one image (that really has nothing to do with Egypt) and one nicely worded sentence. Immediately after an example like this, all of the student groups are fired up to play again in the next round. After you have this system up and running, you can drop it quickly and easily into any unit. Try it with vocab, characters from a book—the list can go on and on.

KAPLA PLANK CAGE MATCH

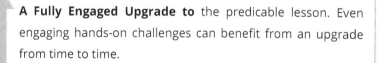

Imagine a World Where: Competing student teams each nominate their best and bravest warrior to step into the arena for a bonus challenge while all remaining teammates work together with their home team to create elaborate structures using LEGO bricks. I volunteer as Tribute!

A Fully Engaged Upgrade to the predicable lesson. Even engaging hands-on challenges can benefit from an upgrade from time to time.

We love providing build challenges for our students in the classroom. For many classes, this can be something as simple as asking students to use LEGO bricks to build a scene from a book, or to highlight key components of the unit. The joy that LEGO brings to students of any age while at the same time pushing them to think about the content in a different way is unparalleled. Thank you Quinn Rollins, author of

Play Like a Pirate, for this idea. But as Ray Kroc pointed out earlier: you're either green and growing, or you're ripe and rotting. And after a few rounds of building activities, even the most colorful LEGO lesson can start to lose a bit of its shine from when it was once a wily and unpredictable activity.

And that, dear readers, is how the "Kapla Plank Cage Match" was born.

Picture the scene: students stroll into class to see that buckets of LEGO bricks are laid out on the tables, ready for them to do the activity they have come to expect. Sure, the energy is still higher than usual, but you can almost see the look of disappointment on their faces after they've done this exact same activity a handful of times in your classroom already. Their halfhearted shrugs as they enter seem to say, "Lemme guess: build the current unit of study out of LEGO bricks, right? Been there, done that."

But this time, before explaining the prompt, you inform the class that each team needs to appoint a captain from their group to take part in a top-secret challenge. You warn the teams that this captain needs to be very creative with building. They really have to be a leader in creativity—and have a dash of confidence.

Suddenly the air in your classroom feels electric all over again, and you give each team about two minutes to jockey for position. Some students want nothing to do with being captain, while others really start making their cases to their teammates, listing strengths and weaknesses as each squad tries to pick the best person for the job. Once the two minutes are up, you call for these brave captains from each team to step forth into the center of the classroom.

Then, in a loud, dramatic voice, you announce that today the captains from each team will be leaving their home groups and the familiar safety of building with LEGO bricks to work together as a sort of all-star squadron in the center of the room using only Kapla planks (which are bigger, clunkier, and far less colorful than their LEGO counterparts). And rather than fighting for the honor of the team they'd been chosen to represent, this newly created superteam will instead be competing against the very squad who sent them to the center! Their mission is simple: work with the unlikely captains from the other squads to build Kapla creations that look even more impressive than the colorful LEGO creations that are being constructed by their regular teammates.

Let the Kapla Plank Cage Match begin!

SUPERSIZED FLOOR MAPS!

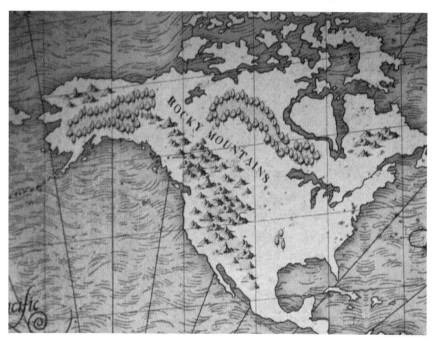

Imagine a World Where: Bigger is better! Our students live in the little iPad-screen world or their 16:9 Chromebook screens or tiny iPhone screens. When we're talking iteration, one way to really ramp up student imagination in an activity is to ramp up the scale of it. I mean who doesn't like a super-sized map?

A Fully Engaged Upgrade to bringing to life a concept or idea in which all students need to collaborate. Whether you're studying the inside of a single-celled organism or the forgotten secrets of a long-lost civilization, many classes ask students to imagine themselves "In a World Where . . . " and this is a great way to do it. The imagination is set on fire and allowed to run wild with this kind of oversized lesson structure.

First the idea. Only certain lessons will work for this exercise. But when you find the right one, it is inspiring to see students work together around an oversized game board! The inspiration here was the movie *Indiana Jones and the Last Crusade*. In one scene, some German generals are updating a large map with troop movements. They have little rakes to move the ships and soldiers and everything! And whether you're playing chess, checkers, Risk, or Settlers of Catan, there's something inherently "powerful" about being able to move tiny pieces around on a game board—what a vivid image to help players feel like they're in control of all the action!

Now imagine your classroom was set up the exact same way.

For the sake of this example, let's pretend you're a middle school history teacher who's teaching a Medieval Studies unit. Perhaps your students are learning about the Dark Ages just after the fall of the Roman Empire, and you'd like them to get a clearer visual sense of the sorts of border wars and resource scarcity that plagued the far-flung kingdoms scattered throughout the European countryside during these challenging times. Here's the three-step activity setup that will leave your students dying to dive right into your lesson plan:

1. Before class begins, you fire up Google and snag a simple black-and-white map of modern day Europe, then you copy and paste that image into Google Draw and add a bunch of hexagons over it. Check it out! It's starting to look like a game board!

2. Save the image you've just made and head on over to tinyurl. com/bigmapmaker and tell the free onsite scaling tool that you want that same image to be sixteen sheets wide. Hit "print" and smile as the site automatically produces a giant map of Europe. (Perhaps you can even task a handful of students to stay after class for a few minutes at the end of the day to help with taping the map together. With less than ten minutes' worth of prep, you are now ready for tomorrow's lesson.)

3. When the next day's class begins, students arrive at our classroom to see that the floor has been converted to a massive, sprawling map of medieval Europe. You divide your class into four evenly sized teams, and instruct them to take their seats at the furthest edges of the board to the north, south, east, and west. Now with students seated in their "home countries," you inform them that each team represents a fledgling warlord who has their sights set on growing their kingdoms.

For the rest of the class, you simply go around the horn as the narrator of the class's adventure, telling a sort of collaborative story where each team adds a new wrinkle to some escalating conflict. One by one, representatives from each "kingdom" have the opportunity to share some ideas about how they'd like to go about expanding their territory as you help them react to the moves made by the other players.

As the lesson unfolds, you continue adding new layers to the tale that your class is working together to weave. Where appropriate, you throw in a few twists and turns inspired by milestone events from your content area, and pause where necessary to work in some real-life history of the region and its conflicts. The story feels organic and free-flowing, and students are likewise given the opportunity to draw new additions onto the class map as they increase their imaginary territories within its borders. Slowly, over time, teams gain resources, make contact with other warlords, and develop into economic powerhouses.

> **PRO TIP:** Have multiple classes? Reuse the same map, and have each group represented by a different color with its very own unique number or (better yet) a name. Then give each group a small notebook to jot down ideas and plans in. This way, they will hand their kingdom over to the next period's group to continue where they left off.

Have more to the story of your course content than you're able to fit into a single class period? Leave the giant map on the floor between classes, and this simulation can create a ton of chatter outside of class. This will get each team's imaginations running with ideas and strategies for how best to move forward with the next stage of their game plan at the start of the next class meeting, and all the while your students will be discussing the events of the previous day while using core concepts they're learning from their time literally spent inside the unit.

Simply put, your students are put into the action of it all. They have true and impactful choices they can make throughout the entire simulation while also seeing it on a scale like no other.

Questions for Discussion

Let's start small and dream big. What might happen if your class sections became competing houses in a yearlong quest for glory? Could renaming something as trivial as "quizzes" and "tests" to something more mythic, like "adventures" and "boss battles," inspire some newfound degree of confidence in your students? Now put your own spin on this activity: what other slight changes can you imagine for your classroom?

If we're looking to create classrooms where students are fully engaged, then we should be talking about more than content. If we were just teaching content and facts, we could teach by reading from the dictionary. Take a look at the verbs at the highest levels of Bloom's taxonomy. How many opportunities do students have to evaluate and create in your classroom?

Sometimes iteration can be as simple as applying a new coat of paint on a familiar staple of classroom instruction. How might using a clever bit of imaginative storytelling in your content delivery help transport students to a world that is larger than life?

CHAPTER FIVE

TEAMWORK AND TASKS

Friends don't lie.

—Eleven, *Stranger Things*

Howdy, folks. Michael here! And I want to share another secret with you. Are you ready?

I love board games! No really. Like, love love board games. Truly—I have over 1,000 different games in my home library alone (we won't even get into the number of additional games I have at school!). One of my favorite things to do with my daughter, Mila, is to walk to the coffee shop in our neighborhood and sit down with a big old stack of board games. We play for hours! And it's always a joy to see fellow patrons raise a curious eyebrow and lean in to ask us what game we're playing. I can't tell you how many times I've struck up a casual conversation or a friendship simply by welcoming a total stranger to sit down to play a game, and I really do think that part of the fun comes from sharing the simple joy of working together to solve a sort of moving puzzle with fellow human beings. It's lots of laughs and a great time!

But for many gamer geeks like me, having a love of board games has historically been seen as a sort of "dirty little secret" or "guilty pleasure." You've probably heard the stereotype of Dungeons & Dragons players gathering with their fellow geeks in their parents' basements, right? Rinky-dink plastic pieces and elaborate rulebooks? Talk about a serious nerd alert! Well, fear not gamers. Because the revenge of the nerds is upon us!

In the summer of 2016, Netflix premiered a sci-fi horror series called *Stranger Things*. Set in the fictional town of Hawkins, Indiana, in 1983, the show tells the story of a plucky group of middle school geeks who, when riding their bikes home from a marathon game of Dungeons & Dragons one night, become the unlikely heroes of an out-of-this-world adventure. Faster than you can say "Demogorgon," our plucky band of gamer pals find themselves face-to-face with top-secret government conspiracies, mind-bending portals to alternate dimensions, and the psychokinetic powers of a mysterious young girl named Eleven.

It was retro. It was weird. And it was a massive success.

And suddenly, Dungeons & Dragons was, like, really cool.

Created by real-life childhood pals Gary Gygax and Dave Arneson in the early 1970s, Dungeons & Dragons is a fantasy role-playing game where small bands of players navigate the perils of elaborately themed "campaigns," as described by the group's resident narrator (aka the "dungeon master"). Armed only with their collective imaginations, a handful of score sheets, and a few bags of funny-shaped dice, these guilds of heroes spend countless hours battling mythical creatures, rescuing far-flung treasures, and collecting magical power-up items. Typical D&D campaigns can last for hours, days, or weeks at a time— or longer—and give rise to near-infinite spinoff adventures.

The popularity of *Stranger Things* was good news for Wizards of the Coast, the parent company of D&D. Sales of the latest edition of the game were up 41 percent in 2017 from the year before, and soared another 52 percent in 2018, making for D&D's biggest sales year yet. Suddenly, what was once a quirky curiosity of the geek zeitgeist had found a home squarely in the center of pop culture.[1] As Greg Tito, senior communications manager for D&D, explains:

> I think what D&D does, it taps into that innate human
> desire to tell stories to each other and listen to other peo-
> ple's stories. . . . Something that was always kind of there in

---

1 Mary Pilon, "The Rise of the Professional Dungeon Master," *Bloomberg Businessweek*, July 8, 2019, bloomberg.com/news/features/2019-07-08/how-to-be-a-professional-dungeons -dragons-master-hosting-games.

the human psyche is now getting a chance to be expressed through the lens of what the D&D rules and mechanics can do. . . . The old stereotypes of what it was are kind of swept under the rug.[2]

Its players agree. As Junot Díaz, winner of the 2008 Pulitzer Prize and National Book Critics Circle Award once explained to the *New York Times*, there's incredible power in team-based activities designed to push the limits of a group's collective imagination. Recalling his own childhood experiences with D&D, Díaz said:

> We helped each other without even knowing it. I learned an enormous amount about what it meant to be courageous and what it meant to be compassionate, and the kind of moral—hard moral—choices that one needs to make in real life in this kind of fake, sort of imagined plane of action.[3]

Here's the beauty of it all: Dungeons & Dragons doesn't depend on fancy high-tech graphics. It's just a fanciful system of storytelling with your friends: "playing pretend" with a handful of helpful rules to guide you along your quest. Simply pick a campaign theme, divide into teams of heroes, and set out to complete a series of increasingly difficult tasks. Themes. Teams. Tasks. Rinse and repeat. Again and again and again. The only limit of your adventure is your collective imagination and the time you and your buddies are willing to spend in play. Put another way: it's an infinite loop of collaborative learning. And if we can get our students as hooked on learning as they are on playing games with their pals? Well that's downright sorcery!

But the truth is stranger than fiction. We live in an era where teachers find themselves ever-pressed for time and forced to confront the unflinching reality of standardized tests (to compensate for that

2 Josh Weiss, "Dungeons & Dragons Had Its Biggest Sales Year in 2017," Syfy Wire, May 14, 2018, syfy.com/syfywire/dungeons-dragons-had-its-biggest-sales-year-in-2017.

3 "Dungeons & Dragons: Satanic Panic," Retro Report, *New York Times*, June 7, 2016, video, 13:13, youtube.com/watch?v=ATUpSPj0x-c.

much-ballyhooed COVID-19 "learning loss"—whatever that means). We keep being told to "do more" with less and less. And when students and teachers alike start to feel isolated, burned out, or chewed up by an education system that has little regard for their personal wellbeing? That's a story with an ending that's a whole lot darker than anything you'll find in Dungeons & Dragons.

Yet we know that collaborative teamwork has an almost other-worldly power. So how can we harness it to help turn an outdated education system upside-down? To answer this question, we'll need to level up a bit of background knowledge with the help of some educational philosophers who've played this game before us.

THE WORLD TURNED UPSIDE-DOWN

Factory-model, assembly-line-style classrooms lived and died by compliance. Certain facts and figures were deemed "essential," and individuality wasn't exactly in high demand when schools were designed to get kids trained up on how to play by the rules in order to prepare for life in assembly lines and factories. This naturally gave rise to those old-school classrooms with rows of desks and the teacher as sage on the stage. Students were expected to sit quietly and speak only when spoken to. And before you knew it, a day in your average "essentialist" classroom looked a lot like a group of children being reduced to no more than obedient buckets who could dutifully regurgitate the trusted facts provided by textbooks, encyclopedias, and unilateral "traditions" passed down from yesteryear. Teach, teach, teach, then review, then test. And we're on to unit two.

In other words? The Game of School.

The flipped take on this approach? The student-centered classroom. You might also have heard this model referred to as "constructivism." Far from the carrots and sticks of yesteryear, this approach prizes creativity over compliance. In a constructivist classroom, things can get a little messy as the student and the teacher work together to co-create meaning in a shared space. While there's absolutely a rule book (or curriculum) to follow, the transfer of skills (like reading, writing, questioning, researching) takes precedence over the more granular details of the almighty content (like the man's name on page 17 of your textbook, or the exact distance from the Earth to the Sun, etc.)—so teacher and student are equal parts expert and learner along the journey. Here, the student takes center stage.

That sounds a lot like Dungeons & Dragons, no?

The constructivist approach relies heavily on student introspection and metacognition, and learners are constantly being asked to explain their rationale behind whatever decisions they are making as they demonstrate their learning in whatever way is most meaningful to them. Teaching and testing are ongoing and embedded to the point where they start to feel invisible, and suddenly the entire game begins to change.

Rather than hammering through pacing guides and arbitrary testing dates, teachers take the vibe of the classroom in real time and respond to students in a more natural, organic way in order to meet them more directly at each stage of their journey. Instead of one-size-fits-none ScanTrons, we're scaling and scaffolding on the fly. Teaching in a more fluid classroom environment, we can adapt to each student's unique performance as it happens, allowing us to offer targeted feedback to all sorts of learner profiles, so that they receive *precisely the support they're seeking in the exact moment that they are seeking it.* In classrooms like these, students are making meaningful choices to find their own way through the learning objectives. And the reward for correct answers is harder questions. It's the same radically student-centered school of thought that led to the brilliance of researchers like Maria Montessori, John Dewey, Christopher Emdin, and Carol Dweck.

Want to guess which educational school of thought works best for a classroom where students are fully engaged?

Thankfully with the dawn of the internet age, it seems that even the most capital-T "Traditional" academic institutions are finally coming around to embrace a more democratic approach to everyday learning. And that starts with saying "so long" to many an outdated system of essentialist final exams. As a 2010 article in *Harvard Magazine* reveals:

> Reversing the default procedure for scheduling examinations reflects a pedagogical reality. It appears that finals are going the way of the dodo. [Jay M. Harris, dean of undergraduate education] told the faculty that of 1,137 undergraduate-level courses this term, 259 scheduled finals—the lowest number since 2002, when 200 fewer courses were offered. For the more than 500 graduate-level courses offered, just 14 had finals, he reported.[4]

Today, fewer than 25 percent of Harvard classes still practice the time-tested tradition of seated final exams where black-and-white "right answers" and "wrong answers" rule the day. And with thousands of schools making the shift to full virtual or hybrid instruction

---

4 "Bye-Bye Blue Books?," John Harvard's Journal, *Harvard Magazine*, July–August 2010, harvardmagazine.com/2010/07/bye-bye-blue-books.

during the COVID-19 pandemic, Harvard is hardly alone. With each new year, more and more institutions are turning toward constructivist models of education, giving rise to democratic forms of assessment such as student presentations, project-based learning, authentic field research, and online portfolios.

We're in the Upside-Down, folks. And there's no going back.

LEVELING UP WITH GREAT TEAMWORK

As the world becomes more automated, the ripple effects of this new universe extend far beyond classroom walls and college campuses. With the rise of educational technology and artificial intelligence making twenty-first-century research faster and more reliable, many jobs requiring machine-like compliance are quickly becoming automated.

The cold truth? Machines will always beat humans in terms of sheer efficiency. With their binary brains whirring away at the speed of millions of megabytes per second, computers are simply better suited than humans for old-school tasks like rote memorization and quality control. Worse yet for those of us "people" types? Robots don't eat. They don't sleep. They don't complain. And they never ask for a raise.

In an era where employees all over the planet now face the everyday prospects of working alongside "co-bots" and machine learning, today's educators need to prepare our students for the authentic demands they will face in the world of tomorrow. Likewise, we need to make it our absolute priority to provide these learners with the very real, very human skills they will need to thrive in this brave new world outside of our classrooms—specifically, by honing many of those so-called "soft skills" that our machine counterparts lack. As a 2019 study from LinkedIn explains, the top five most sought-after skills from today's employers are:

5. Time management
4. Adaptability
3. Collaboration

2. Persuasion
1. Creativity[5]

Fittingly, these are *exactly* the sort of muscles that students learn to flex when working together in teams and small groups when they're creating projects, staging performances, and curating portfolios. Or when they're working together as a daring band of heroes in a Dungeons & Dragons-like campaign.

So what does it mean to be a good teammate? And what does it take to lead a team? Thankfully, we've got some of the smartest minds on the planet hard at work researching the answers to these questions. For example: according to Google's Project Oxygen—a comprehensive 2008 company-wide initiative designed to identify the traits of the company's most effective managers—the ideal leader:

1. Is a good coach.
2. Empowers the team and does not micromanage.
3. Creates an inclusive team environment, showing concern for success and wellbeing.
4. Is productive and results-oriented.
5. Is a good communicator—listens and shares information.
6. Supports career development and discusses performance.
7. Has a clear vision/strategy for the team.
8. Has key technical skills to help advise the team.
9. Collaborates.
10. Is a strong decision-maker.[6]

Hey, wait a second here—that sounds a heck of a lot like the list we saw from LinkedIn. Leadership skills. Empathy-building. Negotiation. Diplomacy. Decision-making. And come to think of it: that's strangely

5 Abigail Hess, "The 10 Most In-Demand Skills of 2019, According to LinkedIn," CNBC, January 6, 2019, cnbc.com/2019/01/04/the-30-most-in-demand-skills-in-2019-according-to-linkedin-.html.

6 Melissa Harrell and Lauren Barbato, *re:Work* (blog), Google, February 27, 2018, rework.withgoogle.com/blog/the-evolution-of-project-oxygen/.

reminiscent of the exact same skill set we saw all those Dungeons & Dragons fans bragging about just a few short paragraphs earlier!

But it's not bragging if you can back it up. And it looks like the science is on their side.

A 2015 study from a team of researchers at Leibniz University in Germany took a closer look at student performance across a series of Massive Open Online Courses (MOOCs) in psychology and computer science—both gamified and non. The results were astounding:

> Many MOOCs report high drop-off rates for their students. Among the factors reportedly contributing to this picture are lack of motivation, feelings of isolation, and lack of interactivity in MOOCs. . . . Students in our experiment showed a significant increase of 25% in retention period (videos watched) and 23% higher average scores when the course interface was gamified. Social game elements amplify this effect significantly—students in this condition showed an increase of 50% in retention period and 40% higher average test scores.[7]

So these gamified role-playing campaigns are super popular, highly collaborative, *and* they help players flex their collective powers of imagination, retain more information, and make lasting emotional connections that endure long after "the game" has ended. So what would happen if we turned an entire unit of study into a living, breathing role-playing game?

The remainder of this chapter will take you through what we're calling a "Curriculum Quest"—a step-by-step collection of excerpts of what everyday teaching strategies might look like if they were rethemed into a massive D&D-style campaign. Are we still going to cover the curriculum? One million percent, yes. But we're going to do it with collaboration. Teamwork. And joy! And just like that, our gamified

---

7 Markus Krause, Marc Mogalle, Henning Pohl, and Joseph Jay Williams, "A Playful Game Changer: Fostering Student Retention in Online Education with Social Gamification," *L@S '15: Proceedings of the Second (2015) ACM Conference on Learning @ Scale* (New York: Association for Computing Machinery, 2015): 95–102, doi.org/10.1145/2724660.2724665.

reworking of old-school standbys like "gotcha" tests, team projects, and end-of-unit exams will feel like students and teachers are having a ton of fun learning together as we go. We've charted out lesson plan ideas drawn from four separately themed adventures:

- History: A WWI-inspired adventure for unit pre-teaching
- English: A Prohibition-era 1920s-themed twist on daily warm-up quizzes
- Science: A sci-fi spin on everyday classwork in small groups
- Math: A regularly scheduled end-of-unit exam becomes an epic boss battle against a comic book baddie

We'll be here to offer a sort of *Dungeon Master's Guide*'s worth of insight from the sidelines at each step along the way. So grab your twelve-sided dice and let's get ready to roll!

HOLDING OUT FOR A HERO

LAWFUL GOOD	NEUTRAL GOOD	CHAOTIC GOOD
LAWFUL NEUTRAL	TRUE NEUTRAL	CHAOTIC NEUTRAL
LAWFUL EVIL	NEUTRAL EVIL	CHAOTIC EVIL

A Fully Engaged Upgrade to those dreadful start-of-unit reading activities where students have to build background knowledge about a particular person or world of study.

Let's Roll: When you begin a Dungeons & Dragons campaign, players get together to make a pair of early choices that will determine what is known as their character's *alignment*. A character's alignment will drastically affect the shape of their entire gameplay experience. To keep things simple, there are two basic questions at the start of any campaign:

Is your character good, neutral, or evil?

Is your character lawful, chaotic, or neither?

Purely "good guy" heroes like Commissioner Gordon from the Batman comics would land squarely on the side of "lawful good" in the upper-left-hand box. Others, like the Caped Crusader himself (who's been known to take the law into his own hands), would probably be more in the "chaotic good" region in the upper right, while folks like the maniacal Joker would surely fall into the bottom-right-hand corner in the space labeled "chaotic evil."

So what kind of character would you be?

Right off the bat, a D&D campaign offers players the chance to make meaningful choices to shape who their character will become. Cause and effect become infinitely clearer. Your choices create powerful chain reactions. And even the smallest decisions can have untold consequences down the line.

Let's take a quick game break to compare this highly interactive character-creation-matrix activity to the standard nightly homework assignment when a traditional classroom is starting off a new unit by reading a handful of introductory pages from a textbook in preparation for the next day's gotcha quiz. Which of these two approaches sounds more engaging?

1. Reading long-form unit introductions with the sole intent of memorizing enough random dates, facts, and unfamiliar vocabulary words to no real purpose other than to survive the next day's reading check.

Or

2. Crafting your very own historical avatar as you set out on an epic quest to battle the enemies and brave the elements of an uncharted landscape in an effort to become the noblest hero or the most notorious villain in all the realm.

Spoiler: it's the exact same assignment.

But one sends kids home kicking and screaming, while the other can leave them practically wanting to kick down the classroom door to see what happens next, as they can't help but find themselves diving deeper into the "world" of your latest unit. All it takes is a few six-sided dice and a blank Hero Builder template!

A HISTORY-INSPIRED CURRICULUM QUEST HELPS BUILD BACKGROUND KNOWLEDGE

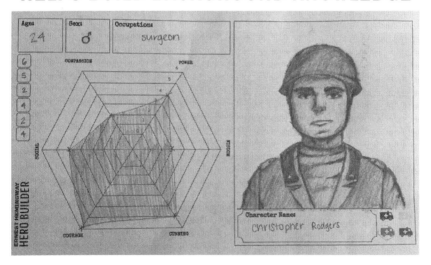

Giving your students the chance to "get in the game" early with meaningful choices informed by background reading can be especially helpful in humanities classes at any grade level. This D&D inspired activity works great when presented in conjunction with a relevant article, textbook passage, or website at the outset of a new unit to help students learn a bit of background knowledge on what's to come. For the sample activity shown here, students were divided into "ambulance battalion" teams of four to five, and asked to review the information contained in their textbook to create a character that might feel at home in a unit on World War I.

Here's how the game is played:

1. Roll six d6 (six-sided dice), and use the six boxes along the left side of the page to record your totals.
2. As a team, use the spiderweb chart provided to determine how you will assign the values rolled on the dice to determine the attributes unique to your historically appropriate character, making decisions as informed by what you've learned from the background reading material.
3. Select one member of your team to use the space provided in the box on the right to draw a picture of your group's character, tying in whatever historically relevant details and facts from the text you feel are most appropriate.
4. Have a second member of the team use the reverse side of the paper (or a separate online document) to explain why your team assigned your character attributes in the manner you did. If your character is especially strong, for example, but lacking in compassion, explain why you made this particular decision, and make the case for how the character's highest-rated skills would serve them well in this particular unit, based on the background information you've learned together as a team thus far. Remember those Bloom's taxonomy levels from chapter 4? "Evaluate and create" are *light years* ahead of rote memorization.
5. Have all remaining team members work together in class or go home to write an original "chain story"—where each teammate contributes a single paragraph using Google Docs or a password-protected classroom discussion board. In your chain story, students take turns giving us a sense of just who,

exactly, their group's character is.

6. The following day, teams take turns selecting one member from each group to deliver a brief presentation (two minutes in length seems to be the sweet spot) where they introduce their character to

> **PRO TIP:** Consider offering teams in-class access to a resource like Rory's Story Cubes, which can be great springboards for helping a group come up with original ideas for their creative writing.

the class. In these presentations, representatives from each team are effectively "competing" in a head-to-head showcase for the approval of the "dungeon master" (that's you, the teacher). Their goal? Showcase the most brag-worthy elements of their group's visual rhetoric, collaborative decision-making, and creative storytelling abilities while simultaneously helping all students build richer background knowledge for your upcoming unit. And just like that, every student in class is practicing critical listening and presentation skills while their fellow classmates recap (or pre-teach) a whole bunch of course content along the way.

This metacognitive activity asks students to justify in-game decisions based on information gathered from the background reading. The beauty of this lesson plan is that it blends super-high student rigor with super-low teacher prep. In effect, it's the classroom equivalent of a coloring book. And excitement is through the roof before you've even begun digging into the day-to-day work of your unit content.

That's a textbook example of some seriously good eustress in action.

> **LEVEL-UP CHALLENGE:** Want to try putting a twist on this same teaching technique for other content areas? What might it look like if we tinkered with the same basic approach to add a little playful spirit to a class on . . .

- **AP economics?** A unit pre-teaching tool to help students research prospective locations for a proposed business.
- **Third grade English?** Drawing ourselves as supporting superhero sidekicks into the world of Captain Underpants.
- **High school anatomy?** A sports science-themed activity where competing teams work to build their ideal "super athlete," tinkering with peak performance metrics so they can thrive in a high-altitude training environment.
- **Middle school music?** A "Spotlight Performer" challenge where rival squads challenge themselves and one another to ask just what qualities, exactly, the best performers need to possess and why (Singing ability? Songwriting prowess? Stage presence?).

AN ENGLISH CLASS CURRICULUM QUEST REPLACES GOTCHA QUIZ WARM-UPS

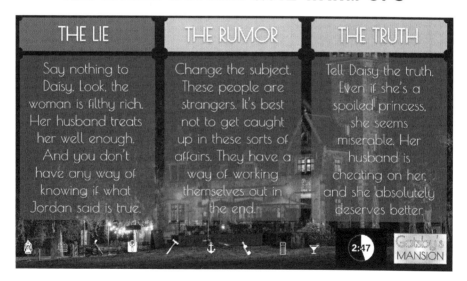

THE LIE	THE RUMOR	THE TRUTH
Say nothing to Daisy. Look, the woman is filthy rich. Her husband treats her well enough. And you don't have any way of knowing if what Jordan said is true.	Change the subject. These people are strangers. It's best not to get caught up in these sorts of affairs. They have a way of working themselves out in the end.	Tell Daisy the truth. Even if she's a spoiled princess, she seems miserable. Her husband is cheating on her, and she absolutely deserves better.

2:47 Gatsby's MANSION

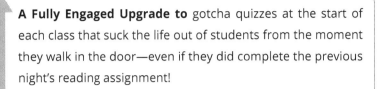

A Fully Engaged Upgrade to gotcha quizzes at the start of each class that suck the life out of students from the moment they walk in the door—even if they did complete the previous night's reading assignment!

Let's Roll: Old-school classes typically start with a warm-up quiz to make sure that students have completed the previous night's reading. It's no secret that these "DIRT" assessments ("Did I read this?") are riddled with problems: too easy to cheat even if you didn't read, too easy to fail if you're simply a nervous test taker, and usually just a collection of low-level "gotcha" problems designed to prove the point that students should have read more closely. But even when these daily check-in quizzes are kept short, there's still no way for students to engage with them if they happen to be stumped. Sitting there for an agonizing ten minutes "thinking about all the things you should have done, young man" is a situation rife with distress—which leads to further disengagement.

No wonder so many teachers call these gotcha tests "DIRT."

So let's put a Curriculum Quest spin on a typical warm-up quiz. Here, we'll use an English class studying *The Great Gatsby* to show how the average gotcha quiz can quickly be transformed into an in-character "Socialite Scramble" where students' collective imaginations sweep them squarely inside the world of this F. Scott Fitzgerald classic.

Step One: The Setup

It's the first day of your brand new unit on *The Great Gatsby,* and students were asked to read just the first chapter of the novel—about twelve pages—prior to arriving at class.

Just before the bell rings, students make their way into the classroom and find their desks in clustered seating with fellow members of their respective "guild." Since this whole unit is themed as a swinging 1920s party, we've ditched the usual fantasy role-playing game terminology in favor of calling each band of heroes a "Socialite Circle" (remember the power of names from Chapter 4?). Perhaps the three young ladies at table two arrive at their desk group where they're given instructions to spend a few minutes before class dreaming up a team name inspired by the 1920s. They tell you they'd like to be called "the Flappers." Meanwhile, those ruddy faced gents seated at table three decide that their squad will henceforth be known as "the Bootleggers." And instead of talking in broad abstractions about this new music called "jazz" that was the "bee's knees" back in the day—students make their way to their desk groups while a background soundtrack plays a few tunes by Duke Ellington and Louis Armstrong to help set the scene. Can you say "enclothed cognition"? If we close our eyes even for a moment, it actually starts to feel like a 1920s party.

And we haven't even started class yet!

Step Two: The Socialite Scramble

The jazz music fades, and the bell sounds to start your class. Our Socialite Scramble has begun. In place of the usual "gotcha" quiz, the dungeon master—er, "party host"—projects a quick prompt inspired by the previous night's reading on the overhead screen. That's right: you won't find any gotcha tests or DIRT at this swinging Socialite Scramble, old sport! Instead, the single presentation slide offers a thirty-second summary of everything from the first chapter like so:

> It's the summer of 1927, and you've been invited to join your old friend, Nick Carraway, to spend a few weeks soaking up the sun and enjoying the company of the newly rich and famous in West Egg, New York.
>
> Tonight you visit the old-money estates of East Egg for dinner at the home of Nick's cousin, Daisy Buchanan. Over dinner, professional golfer and notorious town gossip Jordan Baker informs you that Daisy's husband, Tom, is having an affair.
>
> Confer with your teammates to decide what to do next.

A volunteer from the class offers to read the prompt aloud. And once they're through reading, with a nonchalant click of the mouse, the teacher throws three new choices up to the board. Just like a campaign in Dungeons & Dragons, it's now up to each team of players to choose their own adventure. So, will they:

A. Tell a lie? Say nothing to Daisy. Look, the woman is filthy rich. Her husband treats her well enough. And you don't have any way of knowing if what Jordan said is true.

B. Spread some rumors? Change the subject. These people are strangers. It's best not to get caught up in these sorts of affairs. They have a way of working themselves out in the end.

C. Spill the beans? Tell Daisy the truth. Even if she's a spoiled princess, she seems miserable. Her husband is cheating on her, and she absolutely deserves better.

You set a small onscreen timer as the faint sound of jazz music resumes in the background, and each Socialite Circle is now given five minutes to strategize with their teammates as they search for relevant evidence from the previous night's reading to support whatever decision they might make. What would you do and why would you do it?

As groups discuss, you circulate around the classroom to get a feel for which students are stepping up to show leadership, offer suggestions, or take notes with their teammates. The music keeps the atmosphere casual and you have the opportunity to offer some light clarifications or suggestions to any groups who might get stuck, and you have the chance to mingle among these Socialite Circles to keep tabs on which individual students might not be quite be pulling their fair share in completing the day's work. Sometimes even a quick one-on-one check-in is enough to make a note and offer some gentle feedback if you suspect that a student might not have had the opportunity to complete the previous night's assignment.

Step Three: The Dungeon Master's Debate

Once the five minutes of team-based strategizing have wrapped, you call on representatives from each circle of socialites to take a quick thirty seconds apiece, one at a time, to explain what their team has decided to do and why. Just as we saw in the Hero Builder, this is each team's chance to impress the dungeon master by incorporating some solid text evidence as they make their cause.

The music stops and each circle of socialites watches their classmates' presentations with bated breath. Is their case strong enough to earn top honors? Which team's argument will win the day?!

Step Four: Setting Fire with Fiero

After each team has presented the rationale for their choice, you take a moment to recap the highlights of everything you've just heard. Perhaps the Flappers did a great job of incorporating some serious text evidence! But the Coppers from group four were exceptionally savvy in tying in a bit of real-life connection in their answer with something your class had already learned in the pre-teaching activity about gender roles in the 1920s. It's a close call, but in the end . . . (naturally, you pause for dramatic effect) . . . the winner is . . .

The Bootleggers!

The classroom is a mix of cheers and high-energy head shaking as the winning squad throws up their hands in celebration (game designers call this feeling *fiero*—an Italian word that literally translates to a sense of triumph in one's accomplishments). The "victory" here, of course, is just the bragging rights that their team has made the strongest argument of the day. But the other teams can't help but shake their heads and vow to come back *that much stronger* the next time the socialites come back for the following day's start-of-class debate activity. Within minutes, your classroom genuinely starts to feel like a back-and-forth sporting event where rival teams keep jockeying for the top spot on the imaginary leaderboard. And before you know it: students start reading *that much more closely* so that they can be all the more prepared to bring the fight to their rival squads at the start of your next class.

Heck: you might even up the ante by offering the "winning" squad the chance to call dibs on their first choice of stations to work on for the remainder of the day's lesson plan, while the other teams have to wait their turn. The reward for correct answers is front-of-the-line access to the next wave of questions. But everybody will have the chance to get right back in the game

Notice how high the energy is in your classroom, and the amount of peer-to-peer collaboration and good-natured excitement engendered by this lesson plan. It is likewise worth noting that at no point in these first ten minutes of class has anybody once mentioned a single thing about grades—yet every single student has been fully engaged.

> *LEVEL-UP CHALLENGE:* So what might this same game-inspired pedagogy look like in another course or content area? Why not take this same technique for a spin in . . .
>
> - **History?** A WWI-inspired adventure for unit pre-teaching.
> - **Art?** A *Night at the Museum*-like twist where teams have their say in what they believe is the most beautiful work in all of the Italian Renaissance
> - **Science?** A sci-fi spin on everyday class work in small groups.
> - **Math?** A statistics-inspired warm-up where students work together to calculate the odds of escaping a hungry horde of zombies.

The beauty of this highly imitable "Dungeon Master's Debate" pedagogy is that it can quickly be reskinned to suit the needs of any course or content area. Students:

1. Arrive to class (while themed music plays to help set the stage).

2.   Organize themselves into familiar groups (named after concepts from what you're studying).

3.   Read a single-slide presentation (recapping the key points from the previous night's homework), and then . . .

4.   Set out with their teammates to make an informed decision about what they would like to do next, leaning on evidence from their assigned textbook or reading to find enough relevant details to support whatever claim they will ultimately make.

These "Door #1, Door #2, or Door #3"-type activities could literally be anything that your content area has to throw at them. Make a choice inspired by what happened in a novel. Make an informed prediction about what will happen based on a political decision or business investment. Or make an educated guess about which of three scientific hypotheses is most likely to yield the most accurate results.

Ultimately, "the game's made up and the points don't matter": just have each student be prepared to explain *why* their group made the selection it made.

STATION ACTIVITIES IN A SCIENCE CURRICULUM QUEST CREATE EPIC CLASHES BETWEEN TEAMS

A Fully Engaged Upgrade to old-school stations activities where disparate clusters of students inevitably lose momentum while working in a series of small-group activities away from the teacher's watchful eye.

Let's Roll: You've probably played the game Apples to Apples, yes? Well this next activity is more like "Apples to Oranges," because each group of students will be working on a completely separate activity from their peers, and we'll admit it can be very tricky for teachers to compare wildly divergent work products if everyone is turning in a totally unique assignment in a given class period. Fear not: This activity is messy, but it's a winner. We call it "Station2Station." And it's a lot like Montessori school!

For this example, let's say that you're teaching a high school biology class. Perhaps following a brief mini-lesson from the teacher, your student teams are now free to spend the remainder of the class practicing whatever skills this particular unit will require (e.g., close reading of a scientific journal, interpreting data sets, looking under electron microscopes to make sense of various bacteria cultures, etc.). Like any "real" biological research facility outside of a school setting, there are many different tasks that will all be happening simultaneously in your sample lab-day activities. Maybe you even decide to theme the entire collection of activities that you'll offer for the day to correspond with your current unit (like an eight-day biology unit you call the "Mutant Cell Showdown"). And for each day of your multiday unit, groups have the power to attempt to show what they know at any one of the eight different stations you've dreamed up.

Now instead of having all groups do the same exact task, you roll out a series of old-school "centers" where students teams can select any one of the following activities:

Story Cube Central

Rory's Story Cubes are a themed set of nine, six-sided dice with a different emoji or icon on each face of each die. They're available in all kinds of themed sets (from Scooby Doo to Star Wars!), and they're designed to be a sort of random story-generating tool. With a simple roll of the dice, players can use them to dream up infinite combinations of characters, items, locations, and plots for just about any story imaginable. But they can also be a deceptively challenging tool for classrooms! Simply roll the dice and ask students to work backward to explain just how, exactly, each randomly generated image relates to something that they're currently studying (e.g., "If a cell's membrane was the Death Star, what would be its Darth Vader? Why?"). In this station, the group rolls the nine dice and tries to incorporate each of the images that appear into the real-life story of what they're studying! This one can be tricky! How many different ways can you re-explain the same information?

Sketchnote Scramble

Remember our graffiti pages from earlier? In this station, a team will need a blank sheet of paper and their imagination. Their goal is to sketchnote the most important findings they've come across since the previous day's class. Once again, students won't be graded on artistic ability, but they will need to include detail! So be sure to remind them to annotate each of their illustrations to help a reader make sense of what all there is on the page.

T-Chart Challenge

This activity tests students' ability to use a graphic organizer to keep track of everything they've learned to date. You're welcome to tweak the specific graphic organizer to align with the unique demands of your content area. Perhaps in the fictional biology class, students could fill out a two-column T-chart to make note of any items from a common data set that doesn't quite jibe with the rest of the findings from a recent lab activity. In column one, write each new outlier. In column two, explain why, exactly, this particular item seems to be standing out like a sore thumb.

Socratic Smackdown

In this dialogic conversation station, a small group of students will take part in a free-flowing chat with their teacher about whatever the curriculum has sent their way. Perhaps students at this station are asked to discuss the possible outcomes to an experiment your class just ran and to consider what might happen if you were to tweak just one of the variables that made things turn out the way they did. Even though the dialogue might be hypothetical, the conversation should absolutely be well grounded in the scientific truths that the students have gleaned from everything they've learned in this unit to date. Feel free to pepper the student group with a well-timed prompt question or some "think time" if you ever need to bounce in and out for proximity control with other groups.

LEGO Design Lab (some assembly required!)

At this station, students have the task of re-creating key concepts from what they've learned by using LEGO bricks (or equivalent). Much like the Sketchnote Scramble, they'll be scored not on the creativity of their builds, but on their ability to annotate details of what they've created (by taking photos of their creations and posting them into Google Slides presentations). Maybe students at this station are working together to re-create all of the various organelles you've learned about in last night's reading. What might a Golgi apparatus look like if it were made out of LEGO?

Timed Teacher Talk

Think of this station as your "free space" in the lineup. Where the Socratic Smackdown is designed for student-centered conversation, the Timed Teacher Talk station is really more of a small-group step-back instruction where you'll be able to provide more direct support to a targeted subset of your class. Since having two small-group conversations at the same time can be tricky, you might consider only offering this station OR the Socratic Smackdown on any given day.

Viral-Video All-Stars

They say that one of the best ways to learn new content is to teach it. And this station gives students the chance to become amateur filmmakers for the betterment of your course curriculum. Using Flipgrid, YouTube, or any other closed-community video-sharing service, a team of students has the chance to film short explainer videos of what they've learned. Could you task your students with creating the next great TikTok sensation with a thirty-second video where they create a special dance inspired by what they know about lysosomes?

The HOT Zone

This final station puts your students in the driver's seat and challenges them to develop their own, original higher-order thinking (HOT) questions to really peel back the layers on whatever new content they've encountered. At this station, student groups will be scored not by their ability to answer each question, but by the depth of each question they ask. (Pro tip: you might consider offering some sample questions to help get younger learners started on their way.)

Regardless of which station a group selects, let them know that they'll be working on that station and only that station for the remainder of your class that day. Their goal? Churn out a stronger work product than all of their rival teams at the other stations! And when time runs out to mark the end of that day's class period, you have the chance to review each team's work product to make an expert decision on which team put forth the best overall effort for the day based on whatever criteria you decide.

Encourage students to be creative and try their best, but to keep in mind that these work products are merely a dressed-up take on everyday classwork (aka "practice problems," aka "skill builders," aka "formative assessments"), so there's no need to panic if teams make a few mistakes as they go. Real learning is supposed to be messy! However, the structured, forgiving, game-like atmosphere encourages students to help one another and learn from both their successes *and* their setbacks along the way.

Running eight stations simultaneously might sound like a lot, but remember that you can reuse this same rotating menu of stations again and again each day throughout the unit. Teams tackle a different challenge each day, but they're only allowed to attempt each activity once. So if they spent the day building with LEGO in Tuesday's class, for example, on Wednesday they'll move to the sketchnote station. Three stations down, five to go.

Hey! That's the Zeigarnik effect!

> **PRO TIP:** Not a fan of mutant cells? Take this same core Station2Station pedagogy and tweak it any way you'd like, or choose a brand-new themed adventure that's more suited to your subject matter! You can even create your own customized "dungeon map" by visiting donjon.bin.sh/d20/dungeon/.

When the bell sounds to end your class, student teams will submit whatever work products they've completed. That evening, individual students can continue reading the next assigned pages in your course textbook, novel, or online article. Meanwhile, you'll have the chance to review each group's submitted work product. Which one will reign supreme?

Begin the next day with a quick "medal ceremony," where gold, silver, and bronze medals are awarded to top-finishing teams as you return their submitted work. This reminds players that all teams are competing to submit the top-quality work product of the day, regardless of which station they are currently working in.

What does a "gold medal" win? Bragging rights! The ability to lay claim to the top work product! Or—as a bonus—you might even consider giving the gold-medal team the additional advantage of being the first to roll the dice to select their group's station for the day.

Kicking each new class off with a daily highlight reel of quality submissions allows students to see examples of exemplary work products from their peers. Although reviewing the submitted work might seem like comparing apples to oranges, you as the teacher reserve the right to make a judgment call to highlight impressive efforts across the board.

Your decision on which work is strongest should be based on the skills you've prioritized for the course (e.g., most detailed work, strongest use of text evidence, exemplary use of creativity, etc.). This is an excellent opportunity to highlight those tiny devil-in-the-detail elements that you'd like to see repeated again (neatness, dates on each submitted page, student names all spelled correctly, etc.). It sounds crazy, but there is nothing worse for a team than finding out they've won (or lost!) a challenge that came right down to the wire based solely on the judge's discretion.

This looping process of "create, showcase, repeat" helps keep the daily game close and competitive throughout, and it provides teachers with the opportunity to single out student teams who may have generated higher-quality work products in "harder" station activities.

No more carrots and sticks. No chocolate-covered broccoli. Just a well-seasoned, looping "create, submit, showcase" cycle of lesson design you can repeat day after day throughout the course of an entire unit. A fully engaged classroom in a constant state of flow.

LEVEL-UP CHALLENGE: Ready to level up your lesson design? What might it look like if we put this same pedagogy in play for . . .

- **History?** An American Revolution–inspired unit where each task asks students to earn military badges in the Continental Army as they learn the specifics from different battles or key historical figures.
- **PE?** A World Cup–themed stations classroom where different groups devote entire class periods to honing specific skills (throw-ins, penalty kicks, etc.).

English? An *Among Us*–themed game where small groups learn eight different stations that focus on different facets of editing and peer review (introductory paragraphs, works cited pages, etc.).

- **Math?** A "trick or treat" twist on addition and subtraction, where each dedicated station blends themed word problems with various mathematical concepts.

A MATH CLASS CURRICULUM QUEST TURNS AN EXAM INTO AN EPIC BOSS BATTLE

A Fully Engaged Upgrade to the inevitable end-of-unit exam and all of the painful high-stakes testing anxiety that it inspires.

Let's Roll: After two weeks studying everything there is to know about fractions and the difference between rational and irrational numbers, an anxious group of algebra students somewhere in Anytown, USA, slumps into the desks of their eighth grade classroom for what they believe will be another ho-hum regularly scheduled end-of-unit exam. Mere seconds later, their dread-filled silence is replaced by the sort of energy you'd expect to find at a world premiere of a Hollywood block-buster. How on earth did this happen?

As the bell sounds, their unusually stuffy teacher (that's you!) approaches the seated rows of desks, preparing to distribute their end-of-unit assessment, when all of the sudden . . .

BRZZT! BRZZT! BRZZT!

Every single cell phone in class begins to vibrate and ring at once (thanks to a prescheduled text alert you've cleverly timed to arrive at just this moment using Remind). You fake a quick teacherly scowl of frustration, and gently remind all of your students to silence their electronic devices as our Super Important Test is about to begin. But invariably, one of them raises a hand:

"I'm sorry to interrupt. But we just got a text message. *And it says it's from you!*"

What? Impossible! You're literally standing right in front of the class with a giant stack of tests to distribute. How in the world are they getting texts from your account? Naturally, you encourage students to read the text message aloud. And that's when a student points out that there's no text to read—only an attached voice memo. Feigning a healthy bit of confusion, you encourage them to listen to whatever this mysterious message has in store.

Their eyes light up as a garbled robotic voice (a simple prerecorded message you've made on your phone using a free voice-changer app) rings loud and clear throughout the classroom: "Ha ha ha! You didn't think you'd escape me so easily, did you? Foolish humans! Prepare to face the wrath of the mighty NEGATRON!!!"

Turns out the classroom has been hijacked by an "irrational genius"! And this robotic monster has stolen all eight of the Shards Of Light—so it's up to your brave band of Super Students to recover these numbered crystals that power our fair city!

Working individually, students now have the chance to solve a series of equations designed to correspond with each "Shard Of Light" (aka "SOL," aka "standard of learning") in a row of short equations on the printed page before them. Row one for standard one, row two for standard two, and so on. Once they've completed the work, they call the teacher over to spot-check their efforts. And that's when the dungeon master will reveal whether they've cracked the code with the correct answer before they're allowed to level up to the next challenge. If there's any discrepancy, the dungeon master might offer a brief note of clarification or two ("Oooh! So close! You're almost there!") before circling on to continue monitoring the progress of other players.

The best part: each time a student successfully completes a row of problems, they get to add a big, satisfying red *X* on a massive grid with hundreds of empty boxes that is now projected before them on the overhead board. This one isn't a game of "Student A" vs "Student B"; instead, it's a game of *everyone* in class adding their *X*'s to the group's efforts to lay the smackdown on this metal-mouthed menace! So all throughout the class period, we'll use the grid to keep tabs on how much damage the class is doing to this robotic baddie. WHAM! Three direct shots from Student A! POW! Another attack right on target from Student B! Can the period three students inflict more damage on this tough-talking villain than students from period four?

For the remainder of the class, students watch their progress meters "level up" toward total completion (feeling the endowed progress effect as they go). Players unlock new rows of equations by solving increasingly complex questions and getting feedback from their teacher as they blast each row of defense points away from the nefarious Negatron's layers of armor by adding their individual accomplishments to the class's running total!

A shot of *fiero* each time students receive on-the-spot validation for a job well done? Check.

Fewer stacks of work to grade at home? Heck yeah!

And the power to unlock hidden levels as a reward for students who demonstrate super skills (while helping their classmates earn some serious bragging rights over rival class sections)?

Now that's a game-changer.

Questions for Discussion

Dungeons & Dragons challenges players to think creatively while working in collaboration to outmaneuver the twists and turns of an elaborate story with new secrets at every corner. How might you introduce a story-like layer to a unit in your existing course? What activities do you currently offer in your classroom that could easily lend themselves to a story-like game of one small group competing against another?

D&D campaigns offer players constant opportunities to receive feedback, both from the game's dungeon master and from their fellow players. How much stronger might student performance be in your classes if students were presented with regular opportunities to learn from teammates and opposing squads within the confines of a friendly competition?

At its core, any solid role-playing game like Dungeons & Dragons boils down to a simple case of themes, teams, and tasks. How might you adapt one of these themed warm-up simulations or class work challenges to help students become more fully engaged in your classroom?

CHAPTER 6

FEEDBACK AND FAILURE

*Get a good idea and stay
with it. Do it, and work at it
until it's done right.*

—Walt Disney

Hey, gang! It's John again. I wanted to start this chapter with a personal story that helped me learn a thing or two about how quality feedback can really help you persist in the face of failure.

I work at Bishop O'Connell High School in Arlington, Virginia. For the past fifty years, our school has hosted an annual twelve-hour dance marathon called "Superdance," a massive single-day charity event to fight cystic fibrosis. We bring in live bands. We decorate the heck out of the entire school. Everyone from the fresh-faced ninth graders to the eighty-plus-year-old nuns gets in on the action. We're talking streamers, balloons, T-shirts. And off-the-charts energy that you simply have to see to believe. We have guest speakers who've battled CF. Family members who tell powerful stories of their lost loved ones. And testimonials from alumni who are winning their fight against this deadly disease thanks in part to the collective efforts of our entire school community.

It is quite possibly my favorite day of the entire calendar year.

In March of 2020, I was invited to present at the ASCD Annual Conference (formerly known as ASCD Empower) in Los Angeles. The only problem? The conference was scheduled for the exact same weekend as Superdance. My friend Tim, a music teacher from my school, was also scheduled to make the trip to LA. Like me, Tim was thoroughly disappointed at the prospect of missing the Superdance. But also like me, Tim is a huge fan of the Disney theme parks. And by dumb luck, he also just so happened to have a separate conference in Orlando, Florida, scheduled exactly one week before ASCD.

And that's when it hit me.

Why not fly down to join Tim in Florida the weekend before ASCD? Together, we could hit up the Magic Kingdom. And a few days later in LA, we could even spend that Sunday visiting Disneyland in Anaheim! At each park, we could even set up an online campaign where folks could pledge donations for each ride we rode, with all the proceeds of our "Coast-to-Coast Challenge" to benefit the fight against cystic fibrosis.

With that, I booked my ticket to Orlando, and Tim and I set out for our day in the Magic Kingdom. As soon as we arrived at the park, I took to Twitter to let the world know about our crazy plan and the amazing cause behind it, and folks from everywhere were quick to chime in and offer their insight and battle-tested touring plans.

"Start at the Seven Dwarfs Mine Train!"

"Save your FastPasses for Space Mountain!"

"Be sure to ride Haunted Mansion during the parade when the crowds are lighter!"

Simply by sharing our story on Twitter, we were flooded with an incredible show of support from a handful of Disney diehards from around the globe. The enthusiasm was infectious! So we started posting bite-sized video updates each time we crossed a new ride off of our to-do list of attractions. One ride down, twenty-four to go! Zeigarnik effect here we come!

Sadly, though, contagion wasn't just relegated to those happiest moments on earth. Six leisurely hours into our twelve-hour touring plan, we were a cool nine rides (and one pineapple Dole Whip!) into our first park's adventure when we received some devastating news.

The coronavirus was declared a pandemic.

Schools everywhere began announcing immediate closures.

The ASCD Annual Conference was cancelled.

And Superdance was scrapped.

I turned to Twitter to break the bad news to our supporters: our Coast-to-Coast Challenge to fight CF would have to be put on hold. It seemed as if the entire reason for our trip was lost. The conference, the dance, our fundraiser—all of it was cancelled in an instant. We had failed, and failed spectacularly.

But the feedback from the Twitter community inspired us to change the game.

When I logged into the fundraising app, I saw that we hadn't raised much money, maybe a hundred bucks or so, tops. But as I scrolled through my feed, I kept seeing that dozens of friends and folks I'd never met in person had made small symbolic donations and shared their words of encouragement. One after another they cheered us on and offered warm wishes for our whirlwind tour through the Magic Kingdom park. Tim and I took a deep breath and gave each other that knowing look: "We've come this far already, right? People are counting on us."

The day was already halfway over, and we'd barely completed our ninth ride. But if California wasn't happening, we told the world that we'd be doubling the amount of our own personal donations for each attraction we managed to ride while there in Florida. And if we were going out, then we were going out with a bang.

I posted a new video.

We were going to ride every. single. ride. in the Magic Kingdom before 9:00 p.m.

Within an hour, the tweet had picked up more than a thousand views. People from all over started cheering us on! For the next six hours, we didn't eat. Sleep. Blink. Or use the bathroom. Tim and I hauled tail back and forth across every corner of the park. We adapted our touring plans on the fly as individual rides broke down and new ones came back online. We remained glued to our social media feeds to update supporters on our progress. And we racked up north of ten full miles of footwork apiece, draining both our physical stamina and our cell phone batteries as we posted updates right down to the wire in a race against the clock to conquer all sixteen remaining rides.

We entered the queuing area for Buzz Lightyear's Space Ranger Spin at 8:46 p.m. Ride twenty-five of twenty-five. It was our final attraction of the night.

Impossibly, we managed to ride all twenty-five rides in a single day's time. And we raised more than $1,200 to fight cystic fibrosis along the way.

THE VILLAGE BELIEVES IN YOU

The Disney adventure was a testament to the power of positive change that can be inspired by timely, targeted feedback. In our journey to create a fully engaged classroom—one packed with larger-than-life moments that students will remember, draw from, and ultimately be proud of—we saw something in similar need of change in our schools. It wasn't some rule that was being forced down upon us. It wasn't better parent communication (although we do think we could do better).

It's grading.

We both have walked the path of traditional grading in the past and experienced the pitfalls of that system. We moved onto a more natural system of standards-based grading. "This will fix the problem!" we thought. "We will be completely transparent to our learners about their learning!" So off we went, micrograding everything in a student's academic life. Suddenly, a single test wasn't just one score: it was eight different scores all in one! Questions related to reading. Questions related to writing. Questions related to factual recall ability. Plus individual grades for each of those micro-buckets along the way.

On the surface it might seem like a good idea. And from a single teacher's viewpoint, it just might be. However, spin the table around and take a look at the same feedback system from a student's perspective. If they have ten different assessments in a single class period, and they are enrolled in eight different classes in a single day from PE to science class, that means they are being assessed on eighty different aspects of their learning. In one day. Then add the individual rubrics for any given project at the moment.

This is not only overwhelming; it is downright cruel.

Let's revisit the data on student burnout that we started to explore in chapter 1. Here research again paints a grim picture for our students. A 2019 Pew Research Center survey of teens in America found that 70 percent said anxiety and depression are "major problems" among their peers.[1] The National Institutes of Health reports that one in two kids in America will encounter further difficulties during their school-aged years as a result of anxiety, depression, and ADHD. Drilling this down further, according to the *Journal of Pediatrics,* the most common mental health concern by lifetime prevalence in adolescents aged 13–18 years in the US is anxiety, at a whopping 31.9 percent! We have entered "A Brand-New Age of Anxiety."

While we understand that there are many reasons for this rise in social-emotional disorders, we also believe school, and in particular the pressures of grading, plays a part in this data. Looking again at the Pew data, 61 percent of teens feel extreme pressure to get good grades. Contrast that with only 5 percent feeling pressured to use drugs or alcohol.

So what if we moved from a "standards"-based grading system to one that we call *variable-based grading*? In this model we embrace the

---

1 Juliana Menasce Horowitz and Nikki Graf, "Most U.S. Teens See Anxiety and Depression as a Major Problem Among Their Peers, Pew Research Center, February 2019, pewresearch .org/social-trends/2019/02/20/most-u-s-teens-see-anxiety-and-depression-as-a-major -problem-among-their-peers/.

idea that we will help students along on their journey toward becoming their best selves.

Variable-based grading is more about cultivation than classification, calibration rather than categorization, and investigation rather than inspection. We are here to help move the needle of success for each student. By giving adaptive feedback, self-assessments, and varied instruction, we are truly seeing what each student needs and how we can help them on their academic journey.

As inspirational speaker Alexander den Heijer says, "When a flower doesn't bloom, you fix the environment in which it grows, not the flower."[2]

In order to stem the tide of anxiety, we must help students see themselves as agents of change. They may not be in control of everything that comes their way, but they are in control of how they approach the situation. Then, students will see us not as a road block but as a resource to help them reach their fullest potential. Obstacles become opportunities and trials a chance for triumph when they are empowered. While we won't be there for their entire journey we will equip them with a mindset that will be.

VARIABLE-BASED GRADING IN ACTION

In 2013, a team of researchers from Yale, Stanford, and Columbia conducted an experiment in which students were randomly divided into one of two groups after completing an essay. A few days later, the control group received their graded papers back along with generic teacher feedback and the opportunity to make revisions for a potential grade change. About 40 percent of students from this group took their teacher up on this offer. Meanwhile, the second group received their graded paper along with a simple magic phrase that the team dubbed "wise feedback," a nineteen-word boilerplate which read:

---

2 Alexander den Heijer, *Nothing You Don't Already Know: Remarkable Reminders about Meaning, Purpose, and Self-Realization*, (self-pub., CreateSpace, 2018).

"I'm giving you these comments because I have very high expectations and I know that you can reach them."[3]

The results were staggering: Students who received the "wise feedback" chose to revise their papers at a rate of two to one over the control group. And when making edits to their papers, the students in the second group made almost twice as many line-item revisions as the students in the first! Most impressively, the study found that this blend of personalized assurance and high expectations did wonders for improving trust between student and teacher. The researchers concluded that this feedback was particularly effective in encouraging African American students, as an estimated 71 percent of who received the wise feedback note revised their essays, compared with 17 percent of students who received the control note.

As a social media-inspired sprint through a theme park or a familiar line from Disney's *Moana* might reflect, people tend to work a lot harder when we feel like "the village believes in me!"

THE SCIENCE BEHIND WHY MOST FEEDBACK USUALLY GETS AN F

Video games likewise offer a brilliant case study in variable-based grading. According to world-renowned video game designer Nicole Lazzaro, most video games offer a failure rate of just north of 80 percent.[4] And the game gets exponentially harder as you blast your way through higher levels of play. So, each time a player levels up, they can reasonably be assured that they'll encounter a boatload of failure as a reward. For fun!

Perhaps because in the classroom, barring the rare opportunity for a retest, a failure just seems so . . . permanent.

---

3 David Scott Yeager, Valerie Purdie-Vaughns, Julio Garcia, et al., "Breaking the Cycle of Mistrust: Wise Interventions to Provide Critical Feedback across the Racial Divide," *Journal of Experimental Psychology: General* 143, no. 2 (2014): 804–824, apa.org/pubs/journals/releases/xge-a0033906.pdf.

4 Jane McGonigal, *Reality Is Broken: Why Games Make Us Better and How They Can Change the World* (New York: Penguin Books, 2010).

Why is it that the same student who gets blown away a thousand times in *Fortnite* might bomb so much as a single algebra quiz and suddenly throw up their hands in defeat?

Video games were designed to hook our attention (much like social media). And to steal as many of our quarters as possible, game designers mastered the science of normalizing failure as players leveled up their skills in an endless pursuit of the perpetually moving high score.

WHY IS IT THAT THE SAME STUDENT WHO GETS BLOWN AWAY A THOUSAND TIMES IN *FORTNITE* MIGHT BOMB SO MUCH AS A SINGLE ALGEBRA QUIZ AND SUDDENLY THROW UP THEIR HANDS IN DEFEAT?

When you're constantly living, dying, and learning from your mistakes to be given an immediate chance to try again, the game has created a sort of "magic circle" for SAFE performance where players hit that flow state as they find themselves in a never-ending loop that delivers:

- Specific
- Actionable
- Feedback
- Expediently

Microcredentialing (the act of earning small signs of progress as you see yourself inching closer to a far-off goal) is worlds more engaging than micromanagement (where the teacher has to stand over each student's shoulders to keep them from breaking the rules).

In a video game, feedback is fast and furious and it comes on the fly, giving players the chance to learn from their mistakes and course-correct as they are given countless opportunities to hit the reset button or return to a "save" checkpoint to begin their quest again. Game designers learned long ago that players feel good when they see themselves racking up points (remember the endowed progress effect?), and so they reward players with "atta boys" and other positive reinforcement as they move closer to their ultimate destination. Just like how a high-energy parade of supporters in a Twitter community can inspire you to do something as crazy as try to ride every ride in a Disney theme park before the park closes.

Unfortunately, the same cannot be said for most classrooms.

How bad is bad? A 1996 study by researchers Avraham N. Kluger (the Hebrew University of Jerusalem) and Angelo DeNisi (then of Rutgers University) reviewed some 23,663 classroom feedback intervention systems only to discover that more than one in three systems of feedback actually resulted in *decreased* student performance.[5] That means all those hours we spend providing detailed notes on a student

---

5   Avraham N. Kluger and Angelo DeNisi, "The Effects of Feedback Interventions on Performance: A Historical Review, a Meta-Analysis, and a Preliminary Feedback Intervention Theory," *Psychological Bulletin* 119, no. 2 (1996): 254–284. doi. org/10.1037/0033-2909.119.2.254.

assignment in an effort to explain the "why" behind their grade are more or less wasted.

Either we should give feedback or we should give grades: not both. The evidence overwhelmingly suggests that the second a teacher puts a grade on a paper, students simply stop reading whatever feedback you've taken the time to offer them. Instead, graded papers merely result in students walking away with exactly two questions:

1. What grade did I get?
2. Ok! So what grade did you get?

The Kugler-DeNisi study was just the first of many to suggest that pairing written comments with letter grades is a colossal waste of time. In 2019, a research team composed of scholars including Alison C. Koenka, an education professor from Virginia Commonwealth University, and Lisa Linnenbrink-Garcia, a professor in the Department of Counseling, Educational Psychology, and Special Education (CEPSE) at Michigan State University, launched an even more comprehensive meta-analysis of grading systems and confirmed that *substantive feedback without grades* is the way to go.

As their study published in *Educational Psychology* explains: "Overall results indicated that grades positively influenced achievement but negatively influenced motivation compared to no feedback. However, compared to those who received comments, students receiving grades had poorer achievement and less optimal motivation." In other words, *grades are even worse than nothing at all* when it comes to providing motivation to learn.

The grading game is broken, folks. And when feedback comes buddied up with inalterable grades that feel like they're etched permanently in stone? It's no wonder why so many students' eyes glaze over at the mere sight of all that red ink. And the cycle only repeats itself again and again throughout their academic careers: "I'm giving you these comments because I have very high expectations and I know that you can reach them."

If we're locking each grade in stone every time a student submits their completed assignment, are we really giving them the chance to reach their aspirational best? The next assignment starts from square one! How can a student feel any sense of endowed progress when they find themselves staring at a blank page with zero momentum on their side?

Objects in motion tend to stay in motion. Objects at rest tend to stay at rest.

Pulitzer Prize–winning author Ernest Hemingway—arguably one of the most influential writers in American literature—would famously wrap up a day of writing by ending exactly one word short of finishing the last sentence he was working on. His rationale? The following morning's work would be that much easier when he knew that he only needed to write a single word to already have a brand-new sentence completed.

So how can overworked, overburdened teachers rethink the way we approach the grading game to help provide meaningful feedback and inspire a sense of momentum for our students? If we're serious about designing a fully engaged classroom, we need to become more nimble, more responsive, and more willing to put students at the center of the action. We need to disaggregate "feedback" from "grading." We need to talk the talk ("I believe you can reach these high expectations that I have for you!") *and* we need to "walk the walk" ("which is why I'm giving you the chance to resubmit this assignment, or even the ability to grade yourself based on the gains that you've made"). We must create highly adaptive, human-centered systems of invisible feedback that are both specific and actionable. And we need to lean in on the power of microcredentialing and goal-setting to help students see clear signs of their progress and growth along the way.

Thankfully, we've got a handful of tricks up our sleeve to help you change your grading game!

Method 1: Secret signals help students remain fully engaged

In his masterful documentary *How Difficult Can This Be? The F.A.T. City Workshop: Understanding Learning Disabilities*, educator and disability advocate Rick Lavoie explains that, for some students, the simple act of being called on to answer a question aloud in front of their peers can cause extreme stress and cognitive overload. "What's the right answer?" sends them into a total state of panic as they're suddenly placed on the spot for all to see. But we know that calling on students to answer questions and ask them to share their thoughts is crucial to creating a classroom where all learners are fully engaged.

So how do we get these "players" to feel more comfortable "getting in the game"?

One of Lavoie's strategies is a simple trick originally designed to help students with learning differences, but it's an absolute home run for all learners in your classroom. As Lavoie explains, when he is looking to alleviate anxiety for an individual student from whom he'd like to see more class participation, he'll take a few minutes after class to work privately with them to share a sort of secret code—almost like a Little League baseball coach might teach his young players the secret hand signals that will help them steal second base. He'll then use that code to give that student a head's up that their turn to be called on is coming (perhaps straightening his tie while a classmate is reading, exactly two questions before the particular student might be asked to read her answers aloud). The student sends a quick nod of confirmation back the teacher's way to indicate that they're in and that his message has been received, and the class proceeds seamlessly without anyone being the wiser.

Instant feedback. "Message received." And both the student and the teacher are proud of their secret code, which has set the class up for success while taking the fear and the sting out of that sudden on-the-spot failure.

Sometimes, the best teaching is invisible.

Method 2: Adaptive rubrics keep learners actively engaged

	INTRODUCTION	SET THE STAGE	FUNNEL STYLE	THESIS
INTRO	Introductory paragraph begins by mentioning the full name of the author, title of work.	Paper begins by providing general context of the story's genre, plot, setting, and characters.	Introductory paragraph moves from broadest areas of theme and setting to most narrow area of focus.	Paragraph ends with a thesis statement that is clear and defensible, arguing a position that can be supported.

	TOPIC SENTENCE	ICEE FORMAT	CITATIONS	TRANSITION
BODY BASICS	Body paragraph begins with a clear topic sentence, establishing a central idea that will be supported.	Paragraph flows using ICEE format. Introduce Citation Explain Expand	Quoted content is clear, succinct, and relevant. Paragraph blends both primary and secondary source support.	Transition sentences bring cohesion and thematic unity to the paragraph, often referencing the author by name.

	HEADERS	FONT & SPACING	QUOTED ITEMS	WORKS CITED
MLA FORMAT	Page headers appear in the Last Name [page] format, and are presented in a consistent format in the top right corner.	Paper is written in Times New Roman size 12 throughout, using 1" margins, proper title, and page headers.	Quoted items observe proper MLA format, ending with citations where appropriate, "like this" (Jones 19).	Works cited page is presented in alphabetical order using proper hanging indent format.

	REVERSE FUNNEL	RESTATEMENT	3 EXAMPLES	CONCLUSION
CONCLUSION	Conclusion paragraph moves from most narrow area of focus to broadest areas of thematic relevance.	Paper brings closure to originally stated thesis, restating the claim to offer broader clarity and cohesion.	Concluding paragraph references most relevant examples from each of three pillars of support.	Paper concludes by bringing clarity and cohesion, taking a firm stance on one side of the stated argument.

EXPLORER NAME

TRUST THE ICEE STRUCTURE

LOOK OUT! Every body paragraph must contain primary source evidence and relevant support from a credible source.

JEWEL TOTAL

Carol Jago is the immediate past president of the National Council of Teachers of English and the associate director of the California Reading and Literature Project at the University of California, Los Angeles. She's been an English teacher for more than three decades, but still she admits that there are all sorts of challenges teachers face in helping our students master their craft: "Assigning writing is easy. Teaching students to write is very, very hard."[6]

But what if we could turn individual writing assignments into epic adventures where students felt themselves gathering strength and overcoming impossible odds?

The famed globe-trotting archaeologist Indiana Jones captured moviegoers' hearts (not to mention his fair share of fortune and glory!) by being quick on his feet and staying one step ahead of his foes. Perpetually outgunned and outmanned but never outwitted, audiences couldn't help but admire how this scruffy-faced underdog always seemed to know how to rely on his wits and willingness to take

---

6 Carol Jago (@CarolJago), "Assigning writing is easy. Teaching students to write is very, very hard," Twitter, August 22, 2019.

just enough advantage of the opportunities in front of him as he narrowly escaped certain doom time and time again.

So why not take a cue from the good Dr. Jones to dream up a Fortune and Glory-inspired rubric that inspires students to adapt and overcome whatever obstacles might lie in their path?

Picture this: A tired old "go home and write an essay" activity now turns into an epic quest to recover all sorts of lost treasures from an ancient temple filled with sixteen different chambers to explore. Each chamber comes equipped with its own bite-sized "Temple Challenge" (like including proper page headings or margins) that teachers can quickly spot-check as soon as a student has completed the task. Now instead of just sending students home to write their essays (or copy them right off the internet, or worse!), we actually devote time to helping them practice their writing in class, and give them real-time feedback on where they're stuck and where they're shining. The beauty of the bite-sized checkpoints is that they replace micromanagement with microcredentialing. The check-ins are intentionally so small for each station that a student can simply call a teacher over once they've completed even the most rudimentary of tasks (capitalizing the first letter of every sentence, or using appropriate font face throughout a single paragraph, for example), which can quickly be scaled up to account for additional difficulty to suit the unique needs of your classroom.

And each challenge is worth one to four gemstones, depending on how artfully the young explorer has accomplished the task at hand. The best part? Students are welcome to explore these chambers in any order they'd like.

We absolutely love this idea!

When trying to implement variable-based assessment, you want to both empower students with meaningful choices and support them with non-evaluative feedback throughout. With an "adaptive rubric" like the one shown above, we have taken each element that would otherwise be contained in a traditional rubric and transformed it into a gem-filled "temple chamber." But there are no scary one-and-done scores etched in stone. Instead, a student sees themselves standing at a menu of sixteen different challenges that can help them level up their writing. Now students can select whichever challenge they'd want to try to punch up their submission to "treasure"-worthy level.

Regardless of what individual look-for items a student might be working through in adaptive rubric, and regardless of the individual pace at which they move, its intentionally open-to-interpretation design allows them to see continual signs of growth. This helps students feel like they are making progress toward what feels like a very attainable end goal as they constantly rack up more and more "gemstones" in their individual quest to write the perfect paper. But since everyone is working at their own pace and lightning-fast spot-checking can be given individually as students call a teacher over to review each new checkpoint they complete ("Oooh! So close! This one's looking like three out of four gemstones, Bobby! But you're absolutely welcome to call me back over when you've sorted out those capitalization issues!"), no two students will ever hear the individual feedback that's given to another student.

Believe it or not, that's a really good thing.

Providing bite-sized, specific feedback to individual "explorers" gives teachers the ability to scaffold and stretch the sort of individual suggestions they'll be providing to each student as this "adventure" goes on. But a fully engaged classroom doesn't just move each student from an arbitrary point A to an arbitrary point B. Instead, we seek to move each individual student from *their* point A to *their* point B. So while a student like Bobby might still be struggling with basic capitalization issues, his more experienced classmate Sasha might be cruising through her essay and receiving top marks across the board. This is the perfect time for the teacher to gently pump the breaks the next time she pops in for a spot-check!

To Sasha's utter surprise, she hears that her latest checkpoint (let's say it was the checkpoint about sentence variety) only receives "3 out of 4 gemstones"—a mark that threatens to break her perfect streak record. Naturally, Sasha will want to know just what, exactly, she can do to get that score back up for this category to reach the elusive "4 out of 4" for the bite-sized checkpoint before her. And since Sasha and only Sasha is hearing the particular feedback for this bite-sized checkpoint, perhaps this is where her teacher gives her a thirty-second coach-up about the power of mixing in a few compound-complex sentences; you know, those fancy ones comprised of at least two independent clauses and one or more dependent clauses.

Don't look now, but both Sasha *and* Bobby will immediately set to task punching up their writing.

Using an adaptive rubric like this one, a teacher might give students a week to work on a single writing assignment. This feedback tool successfully empowers students to select targeted areas to address in their paper. At any time, they can bring their piece and the feedback tool up to be spot checked. Focusing solely on one aspect of the tool at a time, teachers can provide rapid-fire feedback, along with the total number of gems that the student has collected in that one step. This is not a graded score. This is a feedback loop! This allows students to head back to their desks and make micro-adjustments to their work. They also begin to home in on specific ways to improve their submissions, and feel a mounting sense of completion as they see that change is happening in near-real time.

Once a student has received feedback, they are welcome to continue to work on that one aspect in order to level up there, or they can explore other aspects of the project by jumping to another "chamber." Over the course of a full week's time, this means that a teacher will look at each student's work several times, from several different aspects, providing feedback and support along the way. And that's not just squishy and holistic; it's super helpful in providing specific, targeted feedback for each student's unique needs. Plus it eliminates the dreaded Giant Stack of Ungraded Essays that all get collected at the same time on the inevitable day when the final project is due.

Because let's face it: if a student was making spelling errors on page one of their essay, are they *really* going to have corrected that problem by page 5 without feedback?

Truthfully, the gems matter as much as a star or a point in the old grading systems of yesteryear. What matters and is different in these systems is that we give true agency to our students while offering valuable feedback for them to create meaningful choices about their learning before it is too late. We are part of their team, not their boss.

Method 3: Lightning-fast feedback with Google Forms

If narrative comments are the wave of the future, and we know that specific, actionable feedback on each assignment is the most efficient way to improve individual student performance over time, just how on earth can we provide the appropriate level of detail that it will take to get all this stuff scored in a reasonable amount of time?

What if we said that you could get something along these lines:

> *Billy has shown some improvement, but more effort is needed. Don't be afraid to annotate your printed text to strengthen your in-class performance! Maintain focus and feel free to contact me during study hall. More attention to detail is needed with homework and at-home activities. Improve Socratic seminar performance by strengthening annotations to show clearer evidence of close, critical reading. Your writing skills are emerging. Now don't lose sight of those formatting basics! And continue to explore different ways of developing ideas and organizing material. MLA formatting with proper citations is essential moving forward. Feel free to stop by for help before or after class. Presentation skills are emerging. Work in small groups is improving, now continue working toward stronger performance in larger class dialogue by incorporating relevant text evidence. Don't be afraid to share*

Student First Name	Overall	Reading & Annotation	Writing	Presentation & Speaking	Closing Statement
Dwight	is doing fantastic work! Keep up the incredible momentum	Exemplary use of Twitter for annotation homework and at-home activities. Creative reflections, with lots of strong annotation and evidence of close, critical reading!	Writing skills are advanced Continue to refine stylistic choices and analysis. Let's strengthen blogging efforts for the coming unit with enriched multimedia like videos and continued attention to aesthetics in web design	Great work in your small group efforts, along with our daily work in teams, your Socratic Seminar performances, and your Snake Oil product pitch! Lots of creativity and incredible effort. Well done!	You're doing great! Maintain that hunger and curiosity as we round out the third quarter. Keep up the incredible momentum!
Angela	has shown some improvement, but more effort is needed Don't be afraid to annotate your printed text to strengthen your in-class performance! Maintain focus and feel free to contact me during office hours	More attention to detail is needed with homework and at-home activities. Improve Socratic Seminar performance by strengthening annotations to show clearer evidence of close, critical reading	Writing skills are progressing nicely Maintain momentum from the research paper to continue deeper analysis of our readings and clarifying argumentative points. Proper MLA citations are incredibly important! Keep this up	Presentation skills are emerging Work in small groups is improving, now continue working towards stronger performance in larger class dialogue by incorporating relevant text evidence Don't be afraid to share your point of view!	You're getting there! Strengthen your overall performance by focusing in on the quality of your nightly annotations, and your in-class activities will reach that next level in no time.
Oscar	has shown some improvement, but more effort is needed Don't be afraid to annotate your printed text to strengthen your in-class performance! Maintain focus and feel free to contact me during office hours	More attention to detail is needed with homework and at-home activities. Improve Socratic Seminar performance by strengthening annotations to show clearer evidence of close, critical reading	Writing skills are emerging Don't lose focus on formatting basics! And continue to explore different ways of developing ideas and organizing material MLA formatting with proper citations are essential moving forward Feel free to stop by for help before or after class.	Presentation skills are emerging Work in small groups is improving, now continue working towards stronger performance in larger class dialogue by incorporating relevant text evidence Don't be afraid to share your point of view!	Let's keep at it and finish strong! Put your power of growth mindset to work and focus on those indicated areas for growth outlined here
Creed	has shown some improvement, but more effort is needed Don't be afraid to annotate your printed text to strengthen your in-class performance! Maintain focus and feel free to contact me during office hours	Exemplary use of Twitter for annotation homework and at-home activities. Improve Socratic Seminar performance by strengthening annotations to show clearer evidence of close, critical reading	Writing skills are progressing nicely Maintain momentum from the research paper to continue deeper analysis of our readings and clarifying argumentative points. Proper MLA citations are incredibly important! Keep this up	Great work in your small group efforts, along with our daily work in teams, your Socratic Seminar performances, and your Snake Oil product pitch! Lots of creativity and incredible effort. Well done!	Let's keep at it and finish strong! Put your power of growth mindset to work and focus on those indicated areas for growth outlined here
		Exemplary use of Twitter for annotation homework and at-home activities. Creative reflections. with lots of strong	Writing skills are advanced Continue to refine stylistic choices and analysis. Let's strengthen blogging efforts for the coming unit with enriched multimedia	Great work in your small group efforts, along with our daily work in teams, your Socratic Seminar performances, and your Snake Oil product pitch! Lots	You're doing great! Maintain that hunger and curiosity as we round out the third

your point of view! Let's keep at it and finish strong! Put your power of growth mindset to work and focus on those indicated areas for growth outlined here.

For every. single. student. that you teach, in a combined total of just about five minutes' worth of work per class section?

All it takes is a simple Google form.

Here are three lightning-quick steps to saving yourself *so much time* when providing narrative comments (for projects, report cards, or progress reports) like what we've shared above. It's as easy as 1-2-3:

1. Create a Google form that only you (the teacher) can fill out, and write one question each for the four or five different skills or areas of focus that you'd like to offer feedback on for this particular assignment/quarter/progress report.

2. Leave the first question with a prompt that asks for the student's name. Each time you fill out this same exact form for each new student, you'll start by entering their name into this first question text field,

3. For every subsequent question, create a drop-down menu of item options with *actual human sentences* where you offer the most frequently mentioned points of praise or improvement that you'd typically expect in that category. Here are three samples:

    A. Great work in your group project. What a tremendous show of leadership!

    B. Good work in your group project. Make sure to ask clarifying questions!

    C. Let's work on speaking up when working in groups. You have a lot of great ideas!

Your lightning-fast feedback Google form is now ready to use. Simply complete the form exactly once for each student by clicking one of the buttons from each of the drop-down menus. Since Google Forms automatically talks to Google Sheets, filling out the form will automatically dump all of the information you type into individual rows of an easily sortable spreadsheet—the contents of which you can copy and paste anywhere else you'd like (e.g., emails to individual students, comments in a gradebook, etc.).

The end.

And to avoid conflating your feedback with the grade, leave it up to the student to assign their own letter grade. Again, remember the mantra:

I'm giving you these comments because I have very high expectations and I know that you can reach them.

To do so, ask students to review the feedback you've provided them, and challenge them to make corrections. After they've done so, encourage them to compare their first draft with their revised draft, and point to specific examples from their work where they see evidence of how they've stepped up their game. Punch up the metacognition by providing students with a blank scoring rubric to accompany your feedback, and ask them to draft a short argument (via video, written post, one-on-one meeting, or podcast recording) where they make a case for the grade they feel they deserve, citing specific examples of evidence and synthesizing the details found in their work product, your written feedback, and the printed rubric.

Method 4: Single-point rubrics take the sting out of scoring

One of the biggest problems with old-school rubrics is how much time teachers spend fussing over what constitutes the difference between a "5 out of 5" and a "4 out of 5." Case in point: A student submits an essay with three spelling errors. Do they lose one point or two? Meanwhile, another student submits an essay with two spelling errors and two punctuation errors, for a total of four errors in all. They should naturally be dinged harder, right? But what then do we do about the child who turns in a paper with zero punctuation errors and ten spelling errors? Aren't you tired of ticky-tack bean counting where two to five errors gets a one-point deduction while six or more errors earns a deduction of two?

GLOWS Strong aspects of your work	OUTCOMES	GROWS Areas for future improvement
	SOURCE MATERIAL: Submitted work product incorporates relevant details from the current unit of study throughout.	
	PRESENTATION: Submitted work product demonstrates professionalism, consistency, and attention to detail throughout.	
	CREATIVITY: Submitted work displays life, vibrancy, and an excitement for the subject matter that invites others to see it in action.	
	HIGHER-ORDER THINKING: Submitted work product demonstrates consistent application of higher-order thinking skills beyond mere fact recap.	

Let's face it: if we're trying to grade everything at once, then it's quite possible that we're not actually grading anything at all.

Traditional rubrics can often be too rigid and unforgiving. If there are five clearly defined categories for scoring and a student does an adequate, if not particularly outstanding job in each of these five domains (say, mostly "4 out of 5"-quality work across the board, with perhaps one rare "3 out of 5" in a particular area where they're still struggling)—we're left with no choice but to crunch the numbers at the end of our grading and issue a blanket score of 19 out of 25: leaving our student with an anemic final grade of 76 percent.

Talk about a motivation killer, huh?

Of course, teachers are often willing to fudge some numbers to ensure that a student doesn't get unduly buried by a black-and-white scoring system if they put forth an honest effort. The only problem there is that we start seeing fluffy and padded grades all across the board where things like, "Great use of lots of different colors!" and "What a creative title you gave to your paper!" start to cook the books. No matter how detailed they might have been, those rubrics become bloated with vague "teacher discretion" bonus points available for non-content standards like creativity and effort. But not every teacher of the same class is always willing to offer these freebies, so kids in Mr. Cowell's class immediately cry foul when Ms. Abdul's students all come home with straight As. And this is where the scoring starts making dangerous departures away from actual content standards as more and more submissions start looking an awful lot like glorified art projects, where the student whose parents own the fanciest color printer or computer software start walking away with top marks.

That's bad news for everyone.

Thankfully, the single-point rubric is an easy-to-use alternative to put in play for any course or content area for learners of any age. Teachers simply present students with a three-column T-chart containing as many rows as there are content standards for the particular assignment. In the center column, the teacher outlines the look-for criteria for each graded component of what will need to be turned in. To the left and right of that column, respectively, the teacher reserves a blank space for making note of where the student's submission "glows" (i.e., the strongest aspects of the submitted work) and for noting "grows" (i.e., those chances to comment on where future improvement might still be needed).

That's it.

Teachers use either the grows and/or the glows columns (alternatively, "met" and "not yet") in the single-point rubric to help learners pinpoint areas where they're shining and where they can still use a bit of work. This more holistic scoring rubric keeps everything sorted neatly into a fixed number of equally weighted categories, providing teachers equal space to balance the good work with the work that needs future attention while keeping all of the comments grounded in the required content-specific skills.

The single-point rubric is an empathetic alternative to the coldly mathematical "4.2 out of 5" systems of yesteryear, providing learners the chance to receive clear feedback without judgment, and recognizing that a single submission can often contain both strengths and weaknesses, sometimes even within the very same grading standard.

And it's even more powerful once you can teach your students to score themselves!

Method 5: Self-reflection raises the bar

We've all heard the old adage that the folks who set goals are infinitely more likely to achieve them, right? Thanks to the magic of internet lore, it's likely that you might have even stumbled across the "too good to be true" tale of a legendary Ivy League study (usually attributed to Harvard or Yale researchers way back in the 1970s) that suggested that folks who write down their goals are staggeringly more likely to achieve them—to the tune of a ten-to-one ratio! Alas, though we love those epic, larger than life stories, we know that the best teaching must always be grounded in critical thought and self-reflection. And when we pulled the receipts on this apocryphal study, it looks as if it might not have ever been conducted in the first place. Whoops!

But here's the good news.

Apocryphal or not, we'll admit that the near-mythic scope of a study that claims to have yielded such radically transformative results is a pretty memorable story, no? You might even think of it as an academic quest for the Fountain of Youth! And when life imitates art, as so often is the case, this epic tale has inspired entire generations of goal-seekers to conduct *actual, real-life research* in its footsteps. In 2020, a clinical psychologist from Dominican University of California named Gail Matthews partnered with Steven Kraus, a social psychologist from

Harvard. Together, the duo collected randomized data from over one hundred volunteers from six different countries, whom they then sorted into various groups of "goal thinkers" (who were simply asked to muse on their future plans), "goal setters" (who were asked to write these goals down), and "goal tellers" (who not only wrote down their goals, but who shared them with friends or colleagues and checked in with other folks regularly to see to it that they were making progress). After four weeks, the participants in the group with the highest degree of accountability (written goals, with written action plans, and regular check-ins with others) reported the highest success rate in achieving their goals to the tune of nearly two to one.[7]

Research makes it clear that writing down our goals, outlining our action plans for achieving them, and sharing this information with others makes us nearly twice as likely to achieve positive results when compared to not doing so. The implications here are huge: if doing something as simple as writing down goals is our first step toward achieving them, it seems as if we are leaving our students with countless missed opportunities for improvement if we don't build meaningful space for self-reflection into our grading process to help them determine the ultimate outcome of each of the assignments we score.

Even if our improvement is only gradual—perhaps even so insultingly small each day that we simply commit to being one marginal degree stronger today than we were the day before—if we make a continued commitment to maintaining this forward momentum, there's no telling what we could accomplish given enough time. In fact, there's even a word for this approach to continuous self-improvement: the Japanese call it *kaizen*. Literally translated, *kaizen* means "change for the better." It's a daily commitment to celebrating what works, while also setting incremental goals for self-improvement, however small they may be. Do one push-up each night right before bed every day for a week. And before you know it, you'll find it no trouble at all to

---

7 "Study Focuses on Strategies for Achieving Goals, Resolutions, press release, Dominican University of California, 2015, "Goals Research Summary," Dominican University of California, scholar.dominican.edu/cgi/viewcontent.cgi?article=1265&context=news-releases.

do two push-ups a day. Who knows, maybe even three. From fields ranging from business to education to physical fitness, this fundamental philosophy seeks lifelong improvement in productivity as a natural outcome of a gradual and methodical process.

In the classroom, bringing fully engaged students into the self-reflective process of their own assignment scoring can be tricky—but it absolutely can be done. Start small. Go slow to go fast. Help your students get to know what it means to demonstrate "mastery" of a target indicator and provide them with plenty of examples to see mastery-level submissions *before* they're asked to turn in one of their own. Let them try on the teacher's hat to size up some sample submissions where the names have been blanked out, and challenge them to sharpen their critical eye when examining a handful of work products that might still need a little bit of effort to reach the quality-control standard.

Believe it or not, these sorts of activities where the students get to become the teacher can be a *ton* of fun! And with practice, your students will start to hone their critical eye and see that they have every bit as much right to make informed critique of work products as the grownups do.

If you're looking to help your learners hone their skills at assignment scoring (and who among us isn't, right? This will save us from a ton of heartache for always having to be "the bad guy" standing between them and the winner's circle), we recommend following this three-step kaizen process to help your students take serious pride in the work that they do.

Step 1: Anonymous

If you'd like your students to get a feel for trying on the proverbial "teacher's hat," it helps to start by giving them an anonymous sample of submitted work to grade. This can be a work product saved from a previous year's student (with the name removed, of course), or something from a fellow student in a separate class section. Since this is the class's first opportunity to flex their teacherly muscles, provide them with a copy of whatever scoring rubric would have accompanied the assignment and encourage them to go to town in sizing up where the submitted work succeeds or falls short of the mark. You can even make this into a sort of mini-game between teams by dividing students into small groups and challenging each squad to see if they can figure out the "real-life score" this assignment received, and why. This is a fantastic way to help students find comfort in the driver's seat while they pinpoint problem spots in a work they know has already received a grade from their teacher.

Step 2: Peer

Once you've completed your anonymous scoring frenzy, take some time to hear from each student group to see what rationales these student-turned-teacher teams came up with to justify the scores they've awarded the sample submission. Compare notes and highlight the strongest points from each squad as you go, so students will develop a clearer sense of what the rubric is looking for and how they can keep their eyes peeled for problem spots in their own submissions. This is the perfect time to provide students with a second round of review by allowing them to work one-on-one or in small groups with their peers, sizing up the submissions of their classmates and repeating the same technique you practiced in step one.

Step 3: Self

Having cut their teeth as teachers and honed their scoring familiarity with their peers, you are now ready to present your learners with their third and final challenge: "Here's your individual feedback from your lightning-fast Google form or your personal copy of the single-point rubric. Can you check this against the work product you submitted and tell me what score you think you've earned on this assignment and why?"

Game. Changer.

Method 6: A rising tide lifts all ships

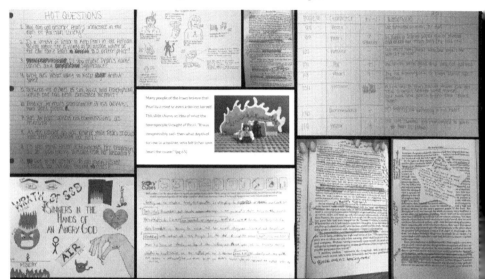

The gamified classroom succeeds where so many traditional grading systems fall flat because novel and cleverly presented new challenges are being paired alongside carefully curated team-vs-team competition. Whether students are taking part in an elaborately themed activity spanning the course of an entire unit or a whole school year, the "game" effectively resets itself at a new checkpoint every day so that each team has the chance to take home the bragging rights of claiming that day's prize. And unlike the dead runaways of old-school classroom standbys—Jeopardy! or the modern day "mash the buzzer as fast as you can" contests like Kahoot!—the steady stream of friendly challenge between squads and exciting twists from the game master (aka the teacher) creates an atmosphere where it truly feels like, each day, it really is anybody's game to win.

Whether your student teams are competing to take detailed notes, create artistic masterpieces, or record bite-sized multimedia presentations to show what they know, something as simple as starting the next day's class with a two-minute awards ceremony where you highlight the best of the best from the previous day's competition can do wonders to compel students to bring an even stronger effort to each new day's class. And if you use the walls of your classroom or your course website to highlight shining examples of student work along the way, you will have created a sort of living "hall of fame" where the young minds in your class start to feel like they're leaving a legacy in co-creating the classroom space as they add their names to the record books for more than just the top scores on your end-of-unit exams. Seeing top-quality work from classmates with such frequency only compounds its effect over time, and the rising tide inevitably lifts all ships as students start to see a never-ending showcase of some seriously impressive work.

Whether you're working on a single gamified day's worth of instruction or stringing together activities to create a larger gamified unit, the tasks will inevitably change as the lesson progresses. But being surrounded by an atmosphere where every new day is a chance to see signs of creativity, teamwork, and progress creates an esprit de corps where even the most reluctant learner can't help but raise an eyebrow and give just a bit more effort in hopes of joining in the fun.

Yes, gamified classrooms can be noisier than their contemporary cousins. But the best part is, you are still every bit in control of the rules of the game! Students work harder because they are caught up in the excitement as they strategize with their teammates and forge powerful social bonds with their peers. We know from Aristotle that students crave purpose and challenge in the work they do, and it is human nature to want to feel validated, seen, and celebrated for a job well done.

In a gamified classroom, teams compete with one another to be "the best" (whatever that happens to be on a given day)—but "the best" is a moving target, and always a relative term that's subject to the teacher's discretion. This means that even if multiple squads churn out work that meets or exceeds the assignment standard for a particular day, the teacher reserves the right to make an expert judgment call or fiddle with their judging criteria *ever so slightly* to see to it that the competition doesn't turn into a runaway that just keeps rewarding the same players again and again. To repeat a line from Drew Carey and the famed improv show *Whose Line Is It Anyway?*: "The games are made up and the points don't matter." And as long as all of the players in your classroom know that the referee's decision is final (and always made to preserve the integrity of the game)—they are infinitely more than willing to play ball.

Questions for Discussion

There's an old saying in education that "the person who's talking the most is the one who's learning the most." This isn't exactly true across the board, but the spirit of the sentiment is well taken when it comes to grading. Specifically, it's the person who does the reflection who does the most learning. What opportunities can you create in your classroom to help enhance self-reflection from each of your students?

Decades of research make it painfully clear that coupling detailed feedback with letter grades simply does not work. How might you use tools like the single-point rubric and opportunities for the three-step self-reflection process outlined in this chapter to get students more fully engaged in the work they do?

Gamified classrooms offer daily opportunities to inspire a novel spirit of competition as teams compare low-stakes formative assessments against one another in a never-ending showcase of daily progress. How might this "rising tide" approach similarly impact the morale of your classroom?

CHAPTER 7

PEOPLE AND PURPOSE

Reading changes your mind,
applying changes your life!

—Jay Shetty

Hi, folks. Michael again. My goal in life is to change the world. Call it silly. Call it crazy. Call it what you will. But it is a goal that has been shared by many throughout history. I think that's the reason I have always been attracted to the study of history. I find it fascinating to learn from the greats throughout time. From poets to philosophers, there are so many examples of how to live a life filled with purpose and passion.

In their seminal book *The Lessons of History*, Ariel and William Durant wrote that "the present is the past rolled up for action, and the past is the present unrolled for understanding." I often find myself ready to spring into action. However, reflection is a powerful ally to those who journey great distances. So let's take a moment to look at the past unrolled for understanding

What propelled any of these historical figures down the paths they would later be known for? I believe it was that they tapped into their passions. Once someone connects their passion with their purpose, it gives them a singular vision, a focus to see them through the inevitable hardships, setbacks, and countless questions. It is what allows them to fail forward. To grow, to reflect, and to take action.

I believe that our passion is for us, yet our purpose is for others.

As a teacher, early on I realized that I would be a better one with the help of others. I began reaching out to a few teachers to meet regularly to discuss what was working in our classrooms. So many great ideas came from these positive-focused meetings that I soon found myself looking for more educational communities. Together, this small group created a podcast, as well as a blog that invited others to share their discoveries. Like welcoming an unexpected guest to a family meal by adding another leaf into the dinner table, we were extending our table to the world. With each new connection came a new idea, a new perspective, and many new possibilities. My theory that we are better together went from a platitude to a philosophy. I sought out more connections to make me the best I could be for my students, but also for others. Wanting to not only connect with but help facilitate those connections I created the Hive Summit where tens of thousands of educators from around the world now come together each year in a virtual summit to learn together. In March of 2020, John and I began writing this book together. And exactly one year later, we launched EMC² Learning, a membership site that is home to hundreds of instructional resources, training videos, community discussion forums, and activity templates that we hope will continue to help passionate educators from all over the planet as we grow, share, and learn together. We once again extended the table even further.

My story for creating change is just that: my own. I am in motion each day to create that change little by little. I have always tried to create positive change in the communities where I find myself. One of the most important lessons I have learned along the way is to invite others to join. While it is important to inspire your passion, it is just as important to empower others.

Life begins with people. We start our journey with our families. They help us learn and grow. They pass down traditions and values for us to be equipped with. Here, our purpose is clear: we play the role of a child, a brother, or sister. We then go off to school and learn our ABCs and how to work together. Our purpose once again is clear: we are students. Eventually we take our first steps beyond our parents' front doors as adults and step into the "real world." Here our purpose seems less clear.

After high school, some go off to college, some enter directly into the workforce, some serve their country, and others serve nonprofits, but through it all, as we seek to discover our purpose, we continue to find fellowship. As young adults we strive to carve out our own path of purpose. However, people and purpose are always bonded together. While each chosen path might find us in different fields of study or different locations around the world, what is similar is that no matter what direction we may choose, we inevitably find ourselves in community with others.

Once we realize that we have always been journeying together, that we are not alone, that we are, in fact, truly better together, we start to see how empowering fellowship combined with purpose can be. People coming together with a focused purpose, an intentionality, is how we can be our best selves. That's right. To be the best individual that you can be, you must look to the communities you find yourself in.

As we pursue our passions, we need only to look at the game-changing examples set forth by our artists. Our heroes. Our statesmen. Our scholars. These figures took their passion and applied it with purpose to change our minds, our lives, and ultimately our history. When one aligns their head, heart, and hands in a common focus, their labor turns into love and ideas turn into innovations. Exploring their stories helps us understand our own stories.

While both your purpose and the people in your life will shift, a lesson we can take from history is that life is opportunity mixed with difficulty. For us to succeed we must tackle the challenges head-on, but we must do so together. Together we travel further. Together we can have a greater impact. Together we can truly change the world. Pull up a chair and share your story. We promise there is always a seat at the table for you.

What do you say? Let's change the world together.

THE PEAK OF THE TIMELESS TEMPLE

Over the past chapters, we've tapped into the awesome power of each of the Pillars of Playful Learning, which help teachers ground their pedagogy upon the bedrock foundation where all of our players know they are safe and supported. Through choice and challenge, imagination and iteration, teamwork and tasks, and feedback and failure, we've witnessed concrete examples of how game-inspired course design can help educators create their own fully engaged classroom. And here in our final chapter we discover that all people can find a home in a space where they and their purpose are welcome and supported. When every learner in our classroom is safe to pursue their passions in communities that challenge them to become their best selves every day, we don't simply change the game, we change the world.

Though the lessons are ever-changing (like the legendary Starman of old), there's simply no limit to the type of creative game-based activities that your classroom might inspire.

As Irish poet William Butler Yeats once so aptly expressed: "Education is not the filling of a pail, but the lighting of a fire."

So let's light this bad boy up! This is the grand finale where we illuminate the night sky with brilliant and vibrant reminders of what classroom gamification is and has the power to be. Think of this spectacular display as a celebration of all that we've learned together, and let it serve as a powerful reminder of the limitless potential that awaits your teaching pedagogy.

The fully engaged classroom always offers:

- Choice and challenge
- Imagination and iteration
- Teamwork and tasks

- Feedback and failure
- And finally . . . people and purpose.

PLAYING WITH PURPOSE

Antoine de Saint-Exupéry was a French writer, poet, and pioneering aviator. He became a laureate of several of France's highest literary awards, and was the recipient of the prestigious National Book Award in the US. He is known for his beloved novella *Le Petit Prince—The Little Prince*—a charming philosophical fable about a young boy who finds himself the unlikely hero of a fantastic voyage across the universe and through the furthest reaches of his imagination. But his explorer's spirit is perhaps best encapsulated in the following quote, which has long been attributed to his name:

> If you want to build a ship, don't drum up the men to gather wood, divide the work and give orders. Instead, teach them to yearn for the vast and endless sea.[1]

---

1 jobs.netflix.com/culture

"Teach them to yearn for the vast and endless sea." What a marked departure this sentiment is from the usual grade-focused trajectory that we so often see in countless classrooms around the globe.

We want our students to think like historians. To question the world critically and analytically with the insight of scientists and mathematicians. To savor the beauty and power of the written word. To pursue physical fitness and the arts not for a paycheck but simply for the love of peak performance. To value truth and seek veracity in what they read, write, and research. We want our students to yearn for the vast and endless rewards that await them in rich and authentic lessons long after our time together in the classroom has ended, as they become lifelong learners.

But far too often, our classroom "purpose" simply amounts to the exact opposite of such intentionality.

"Complete this homework in order to get a grade."

"Turn in your notes to prove you were listening."

"Copy down what I wrote on the board because it will be on the test."

"Memorize these facts before Thursday's quiz."

"Get a good grade on this assignment so you can get into a good college."

Consequently, our students inevitably cut corners. They cheat. They concede failure. And far too often, they simply check out. They stop yearning for the vast and endless sea altogether. And once that happens, teachers inevitably return to what Brazilian educator Paulo Freire famously derided as the "banking" model of education. In layman's terms: you do this and you get that. In his watershed 1968 text, *Pedagogy of the Oppressed*, Freire explains:

> Narration (with the teacher as narrator) leaves the students to memorize mechanically the narrated content. Worse yet, it turns them into "containers," into "receptacles" to be "filled" by the teacher. The more completely she fills the receptacles, the better a teacher she is. The more

meekly the receptacles permit themselves to be filled, the better students they are.

Education thus becomes an act of depositing, in which the students are the depositories and the teacher is the depositor. Instead of communicating, the teacher issues communiques and makes deposits which the students patiently receive, memorize, and repeat. This is the banking concept of education, in which the scope of action allowed to the students extends only as far as receiving, filing, and storing the deposits. They do, it is true, have the opportunity to become collectors or cataloguers of the things they store. But in the last analysis, it is the people themselves who are filed away through the lack of creativity, transformation, and knowledge in this (at best) misguided system. For apart from inquiry, apart from the praxis, individuals cannot be truly human. Knowledge emerges only through invention and reinvention, through the relentless, impatient, continuing, hopeful inquiry human beings pursue in the world, with the world, and with each other.[2]

Freire explains that such leaders "do not organize the people—they manipulate them. They do not liberate, nor are they liberated: they oppress." A truly radical leader, according to Freire, fully surrenders to working for the good of those whom they seek to serve. We don't pretend to know what's best for our students. We listen to them. We replace thoughts of "What's the matter with you?" with the question of "What matters *to you*?"

If we want the people in our charge to pursue *their* purpose, then we need to stop designing classrooms as spaces where we are imposing *our* decisions.

This subtle shift can truly change the world.

---

2 Paulo Freire, *Pedagogy of the Oppressed: 50th Anniversary Edition*, trans. Myra Bergman Ramos (New York: Bloomsbury Academic, 2018).

In the spring of 2019, more than 10,000 teachers gathered in Chicago, Illinois, for the ASCD Annual Conference, one of the largest education conferences in the country. The keynote speaker for the closing session was Ashton Kutcher—yes, *that* Ashton Kutcher—the tall, good-looking actor from *That '70s Show* and such timeless cinema classics as *Dude, Where's My Car?* But Ashton Kutcher is much more than a Hollywood A-lister. He was the first person in the world to gain more than one million Twitter followers. He is a venture capitalist who oversees the daily operations of a $250 million company that invests heavily in tech startups, including Spotify, Airbnb, and Uber. And above all else, he is a devoted philanthropist and advocate for victims' rights. In 2009, he founded a nonprofit called Thorn, an international anti-human-trafficking organization dedicated to the protection of children around the world. And in 2017, Kutcher's nonprofit work led him to testify before the Senate Foreign Relations Committee, where he explained how Thorn is partnering with cutting-edge tech giants like Facebook, Microsoft, and Google to create a massive database to support millions of child abuse victims all across the web.

In short, Ashton Kutcher is more than just a pretty face, and he's more than willing to put his money where his mouth is. Perhaps it's no wonder that *Time* magazine once counted him as one of its one hundred most influential people on the planet.

When asked at the 2019 ASCD Annual Conference what advice he had for educators, Kutcher said that he thinks most schools are "abysmal" at teaching children to discover their own purpose. He continued

IF WE WANT THE PEOPLE IN OUR CHARGE TO PURSUE THEIR PURPOSE, THEN WE NEED TO STOP DESIGNING CLASSROOMS AS SPACES WHERE WE ARE IMPOSING OUR DECISIONS.

by explaining that "we ask kids to do so many things in our classrooms, but we never really let them figure out the kind of person that they want to be." After a moment's pause, Kutcher added, "I never really felt comfortable being vulnerable with any of my teachers, because they were never really vulnerable with me."

In Kutcher's estimation, schools need to facilitate pathways for students to find their purpose, and they need to stop telling these learners what other people mechanically expect their purpose to be. This recalls the lifelong commitment to reinvention we saw from David Bowie. It echoes all sorts of modern day educational buzz terms like "choice and voice," "student-centered classrooms," and "self-guided learning." It likewise follows the timeless education models championed by Paulo Freire, Maria Montessori, John Dewey, and Socrates himself.

ASK QUESTIONS. DON'T BE AFRAID OF MESSY ANSWERS. AND CHALLENGE STUDENTS TO FIND THE DEEPER MEANING BEHIND THE THINGS THAT THEY VALUE.

Ask questions. Don't be afraid of messy answers. And challenge students to find the deeper meaning behind the things that they value.

For Ashton Kutcher, he found his purpose when he discovered acting—which immediately made sense of all the setbacks he'd encountered along the way. "Once you have purpose," he explained, "failure becomes an inevitability on the way to fulfillment."

Gamification helps students recognize a clear goal for each day's efforts while taking the sting out of getting an answer or two wrong in our ultimate journey toward reaching a tangible goal that's always just one step closer to being within our reach. It establishes clear beacons for aspirational achievement, and provides frequent signposts to celebrate a learner's success. If we want our students to become fully engaged, we need to incentivize effort.

Not being "right." And that's what the best games do: respond to our best efforts by providing us with new challenges. Beating level one only to discover all the possibilities that await us in level two. Honing our skills in rec league until we're ready to play at the junior varsity level, and then inspiring us to move up from the JV squad to the varsity team and beyond.

Redesigning our classrooms so that they are more playful, more game-like, and more fully engaged results in a learning environment where all of the people in our charge feel like partners on the same team, working together with the shared purpose of tackling a common goal. Borrowing elements from well-designed games allows us to offer faster feedback. Powerful team-based play. Immersive themes. Richer choice. More personalized challenge. Imagination. Iteration. Once we understand and value the things held dear by the students we serve, we can help them see how these things connect to the classes we teach. But this is not some sort of lip service: We do it by humbling ourselves. By recognizing the need to shake the very foundations of what school has become to rebuild what school could and should be. And we do it by allowing ourselves to become vulnerable.

In a fully engaged classroom, the line between teacher and student can often be a blurry one. True liberation can only occur when learners and leaders share the humility and resolve to join side by side and work together as teammates in pursuit of a common goal. Our purpose is clear: every one of us is here to learn. As we learned from Socrates, questions are just as rewarding as answers. In this classroom, no one will walk in or walk out pretending that they have all the answers. And today's class will be fundamentally different simply because each one of us has shown up to give it our very best. Of course, the obstacles will inevitably get harder as we progress. But we are all on the same team.

The game is ever new and ever changing.

A PARTING CHECKLIST

Before we leave our stay in this Timeless Temple, we wanted to offer you a brief checklist to help find your way back here at any time. If you're looking for a more detailed map toward this playful approach to a fully engaged classroom, you are certainly welcome to retrace your steps through any of the preceding chapters at any time. But if you're looking for a faster and more itemized list of takeaways when developing new lessons to serve the unique group of people and purposes that your classroom might have to offer, we think this checklist can serve as a powerful reminder of everything that we've explored and discovered up until this point. The rest of the adventure is entirely up to you!

FULLY ENGAGED CLASSROOM: THE CHECKLIST

Start with vulnerability

If we want our students to be vulnerable with us, then we need to feel comfortable being vulnerable with them. This doesn't mean that we have to pour our hearts out or share every last detail of our life stories to the children in our charge. But it absolutely does mean that we need to drop the whole know-it-all act and invite our students into a classroom world where they feel empowered to become co-creators of their learning. This is the first step to creating a classroom that's fully engaged.

In a school environment where the only "purpose" is to get the highest grade, when students get so much as a single review question wrong, they are far too regularly willing to throw their hands up and surrender. Yet later that day, they'll spend countless hours on the playing field or in a video game, routinely missing hundreds of shots on the way toward leveling up their talents.

Because, when you're playing a sport or a game outside of class, the purpose is immediately clear. You want to be the best. And the game encourages you to keep trying, even when you're feeling stuck.

As Wayne Gretzky once said (or was it Michael Scott?): "You miss 100 percent of the shots you don't take."

This can start with a simple question to your students. "What two emotions are you feeling today?" "What sorts of things do you enjoy doing outside of the classroom?" Listen to what they have to say. Then go home and see if you can reverse engineer design elements from these same activities to put them in play in your classroom. You don't have to understand every last nuance of *Fortnite* or *Call of Duty* to connect with your students. But learning from the emotional triggers that make these games so resonant with them will absolutely make your classroom just as addictive.

Perhaps students enjoy the feeling of teamwork or comradery as they dig deep to accomplish some impossible challenge. Or they savor the opportunity to unlock new pathways and hidden secrets. Maybe they love seeing colorful badges or awards for a job well done. Whatever it is that sparks your learners' interests: discover it as soon as you can, and tap into its power to transform your classroom.

Give yourself permission

Call it a product of habit, routine, or well-reasoned trepidation, but from the moment we set foot in our classrooms, so many teachers feel the need to follow the same trodden paths that led them through their own education. Occasionally, we replace one book here or there with a more timely or suitable replacement. Or we take what once was a thirty-question multiple choice test and knock it down to twenty questions and a short essay. But these gradual reforms rarely result in any major curricular or pedagogical changes. And as a result, so many teachers find themselves frustrated by the process as each new generation of students turns on, tunes in, and drops out.

In case no one has ever told you this before, it probably bears saying outright: give yourself permission to change the game.

In chapter 1, we talked about the fictional story of Ms. Jones and Mr. Smith. But you're neither of those teachers, are you? So stop trying to keep up with the Joneses! Your goal as a teacher is to be *your* best self—students recognize teachers who lead with authenticity and vulnerability in an effort to bring their very best each day in the classroom. Don't wear yourself out trying to be the carbon copy of the cool new guy down the hall or the heir apparent to a thirty-year educator who swears she knows all there is to know about your school's time-honored curriculum. Do you know how those "beloved" teachers came to be so fondly remembered by their students? Not by pretending to be someone they are not. By being themselves. No pretext. No put-ons. And no hiding who they really are.

This echoes the sentiment from our first bullet point: figure out the things that set *your* soul on fire! Then find a way to capture that same spirit in your classroom. If you love the thrill of a buzzer-beater or a last-second walk-off home run, find a way to create classroom competitions that leave students on the edge of their seats right up until those heart-stopping final moments when the game comes down to the wire! If you're a geek for reality TV shows where someone gets eliminated after a grueling head-to-head showdown, borrow elements from those programs to up the ante. Create "must see" lessons where students won't want to miss what happens next. If you're a card collector, a devotee of national parks, a die-hard fan of comic books—you name it! Give yourself permission to tap into your passion and invite students to come along for the ride. When principals notice that students are taking part in high-energy classroom activities full of rigor, relevance, and authentic engagement, they almost always respond by encouraging their teachers to keep up the great work.

Keep feelings first

Great games start by asking what they want players to feel before the game designers ever set up what, exactly, they'll challenge players to do. A game like Monopoly sets out to elicit feelings of power and dominance when you win (and soul-deadening despair when you fall behind). A game like Clue challenges you to outwit and out-sleuth your rivals in an elaborate game of misdirection, red herrings, and top-secret fact-finding in order to elicit feelings of pride and intelligence. And a game like *Mario Kart* offers a string of colorful explosions and a welcome parade of power-ups in a quest to battle against one's buddies in a highly social showdown designed to reward the most clever and resourceful player in all the land.

Do the same thing in your classroom activity design. What do you want your students to *feel* in this lesson? What choices and challenges can you present them to make sure that this feeling is sustained throughout your class period and beyond? Long after they forget any of the incidental details they encounter along the way, do you want them to walk away from this class feeling curious? Empowered? Ready to fight against injustice? Thinking about creative ways to apply known formulas to tackle authentic problems outside of your classroom? Let this feeling serve as the beating heart of your lesson design. And put your students in the driver's seat.

Feedback and iteration

Motivational speaker Jim Rohn famously said that we are the average of the five people we spend the most time with.[3] If that's true, it might also be said that the fire that we bring to our work inside the classroom is every bit as much the average of the five teachers we surround ourselves with, the five most recent pedagogical books or podcasts or vlogs we consumed, or even the five non-school-related passions to which we devote ourselves so freely in our time outside of it. So give yourself permission to steal teaching ideas from your favorite reality television program. Ask your students what, exactly, their latest video game is challenging them to do—and how it offers them positive feedback when they see signs of their progress toward some far-off goal. Watch your favorite sporting event and see if you can capture the intangible quality that compels fans to sit on the edge of their seats right up until

---

3 Aimee Groth, "You're The Average Of The Five People You Spend The Most Time With," Business Insider, July 24, 2012, businessinsider.com/jim-rohn-youre-the-average-of-the-five-people-you-spend-the-most-time-with-2012-7#:~:text=David%20P%20Brown%20Motivational%20speaker,the%20average%20of%20all%20outcomes.

the final buzzer sounds. Then, using what you've learned, try coopting a handful of these same motivational strategies into your classroom.

Whether you love yoga, baseball, painting, or professional dance, think about just how much education has in common with these other performance-based activities. Is it any wonder, then, why it's called a teaching "practice?" In each unique realm, you'll encounter die-hards and devotees who throw themselves into their craft with unrivaled zeal. When you know the purpose of the work you do, obstacles are only stepping stones. You got this! Now go and get it.

This is the radical power of the fully engaged classroom. A place of wonder. Curiosity. Good-natured competition. Choice. Challenge. *Fiero.* Flow. Discovery. Passion. Intentionality. And a whole lot of fun. It is, in the immortal words of the game-changing Starman David Bowie himself, a place where we can "let all the children boogie."

We embrace our inner "rebel rebels" and recognize that the students are, were, and should always remain the heroes of our classrooms. Our students become the brilliant, beautiful forces of nature that each of them were born to be. Forces for inclusion. For empathy. And forces for change. That's how we preserve the Timeless Temple for generations to come.

Indeed, when we turn and face the strange, that's how we ch-ch-change the world.

Questions For Discussion

As we started this chapter, we suggested that our passion is for us, yet our purpose is for others. What is your passion? And how might gamified instruction help you channel that passion into your classroom? What is your purpose? Are you a teacher of content or a teacher of people?

The closing pages of this chapter were designed to feel like a spectacular fireworks display at the grand finale of an epic adventure that left you feeling empowered, inspired, and excited to change the game in your teaching practice. What is one thing that you can take away from this high-energy hit parade to make your classroom more fully engaged, starting with the next time you set foot in your school building?

Gamified instruction has helped each of us change the game in our classrooms, but our goal is to extend this teachers' table to as many educators as would like to join in the fun. Our combined purpose is not just to help teachers change the game, but to help them change the world. What is the one thing in this book that has resonated with you the most to help you in your journey to be an agent for change? Tweet us @MrMatera or @MeehanEDU and use the hashtag #EMC2Learning to let us know!

GAME ON!

As our journey through the Timeless Temple draws to a close, we can't help but marvel at just how far we've progressed from that Page-Nine Ending you'll remember from early on. Together, we've seen just how much a fully engaged classroom shares in common with a really great game. The pleasure centers in our brains flood with possibilities from the moment we sit down to play. It can captivate our attention! It can get pretty loud! It's often messy. It's rarely linear. And there are a billion ways to play it again and again and again.

And that's what makes it such a blast to return to. Every. Single. Day.

And one more thing! Our "Choose Your Own ED-venture" still has one final surprise in store. Congratulations! You've unlocked the Last-Page Ending:

THE LAST-PAGE ENDING

It's Monday morning and you can't wait to set foot inside your school. You've just started a brand new unit where you've put your own unique spin on the game-inspired teaching techniques you discovered in the Legendary Lake of Learning and the Timeless Temple, and students have been blowing up your inbox all weekend with curiosity at what adventures might await them in today's lesson! Their energy levels have been through the roof over these past few weeks. They're creating. Collaborating. Imagining. Pushing one another to work harder! And forging ahead no matter what obstacles lie in their path. You've never seen this kind of enthusiasm for school before. And you're so eager to beat them into the classroom that you even forgot your trusty travel mug on the kitchen countertop this morning.

But, no time for coffee! You feel that electricity in the air and your skin starts to prickle with excitement at all the possibilities of what could be. Your classroom is fully engaged. And today is going to be a game-changer.

Breezing past your teacher mailbox before the first bell rings, you run into Geoff.

"Ugh. Mondays. Am I right?" he says with a frown.

Before you can answer, he begins to tell you how he's giving a big test today, yet his students have all but checked out. Between the behavior and the grading and the lesson planning, he's exhausted. And ready to throw in the towel.

You smile at your friend.

"Hey, Geoff. You know, I'd love for you to come by my room today during your prep. I've got something I think you'd really love to see . . . "

From the bottom of our hearts, we thank you for joining us on this epic adventure. And we warmly invite you to give us a shout on Twitter by dropping a line to @MrMatera or @MeehanEDU, or use the hashtag

#EMC2Learning. We'd love to hear your insight on the book and continue the conversation on ways that we might be able to support you. Please let us know your thoughts! And keep asking questions! As a wise man once said . . .

"Hmmm. Very interesting! And why do you think that?"

Michael Matera and John Meehan
Milwaukee, Wisconsin & Washington, DC, spring 2021

ABOUT THE AUTHORS

 Michael Matera | @MrMatera

Ciao, everyone! I am Michael. I have been a teacher and learner all over this world. From my studies in Korea and Rome to my teaching in Milan, Italy, to Milwaukee, Wisconsin, I am a lifelong learner through and through. For the past twelve years, I have had the absolute pleasure of teaching at University School of Milwaukee as a middle school world history teacher, and as a published author and keynote speaker. I have presented around the United States.

But that's not all I am. First and foremost, I am a father. Second, a foodie (I mean, remember Maslow's hierarchy of needs), and third, I am a nerd. My educational philosophy could best be summed up by a Cesare Pavese quote: "We don't remember days, we remember moments." I think we as teachers can create moment-filled classes that can literally change the trajectory for our students, and as such, we can change the world.

I couldn't be more excited to join with John, my close friend and game-changer, to change the world together! He is a dynamic educator who pours his heart into whatever communities he finds himself in. Lucky for us, one of those communities happens to be education. Our message is a simple one: making moments makes memories. And nothing does that better than the ideas we have shared in our first joint effort. John and I believe we are all better together.

In life, the most important things we do, we do together. So let's get busy changing the world!

John Meehan | @MeehanEDU

Hey folks! I'm John. These days, I'm an eleventh grade English teacher and an instructional coach at a Catholic high school in Northern Virginia. I started my teaching career a little over a decade ago in the public schools in and around my adopted hometown of Washington, DC. When I'm not teaching or presenting, I'm also a marathoner. A Spartan. A Tough Mudder. A die-hard fan of the New England Patriots. And a serious theme-park junkie. I believe that enthusiasm is infectious, and that our classrooms should feel like a full-blown escape from the everyday routine of the time-honored academic death march.

They say your favorite class is the one that you like the most. And your best class is the one where you learn the most. I want my class to be both.

Every.

Single.

Day.

In 2019, I published a book called *EDrenaline Rush: Game-Changing Student Engagement Inspired by Theme Parks, Mud Runs, and Escape Rooms.* I think that great classrooms can borrow so much from these high-energy spectacles of fun and excitement. Our students are hungry to learn! If we can spark their curiosity, I sincerely believe that there is no limit to what we can achieve. And in that same spirit of innovation and wonder, I am over the moon to join forces with Michael in this project. Not only is he a serious gamer, he is a brilliant educator, a thoughtful writer, and an even better friend. I simply cannot wait to show you all of the cool new stuff that we've come up with together in this book to help you change the game in your classroom!

Final Note: Don't forget that we offer an entire website where teachers from around the world join together to change the Game of School. **EMC2Learning.com** is an online library of student engagement strategies, bite-sized PD tutorials, and fully editable classroom resources. There's no fancy software to install or work-sheets to copy. Just one massive 24/7 membership community with discussion forums, instructional videos, and hundreds of high-energy classroom activities to choose from—all intentionally designed to be content agnostic so they can quickly be scaled and modified for any curriculum, grade level, or content area.

MORE FROM

Since 2012, DBCI has published books that inspire and equip educators to be their best. For more information on our titles or to purchase bulk orders for your school, district, or book study, visit **DaveBurgessConsulting.com/DBCIbooks**.

More from the Like a PIRATE™ Series
Teach Like a PIRATE by Dave Burgess
eXPlore Like a PIRATE by Michael Matera
Learn Like a PIRATE by Paul Solarz
Play Like a PIRATE by Quinn Rollins
Run Like a PIRATE by Adam Welcome
Tech Like a PIRATE by Matt Miller

Lead Like a PIRATE™ Series
Lead Like a PIRATE by Shelley Burgess and Beth Houf
Balance Like a PIRATE by Jessica Cabeen, Jessica Johnson, and Sarah Johnson
Lead beyond Your Title by Nili Bartley
Lead with Appreciation by Amber Teamann and Melinda Miller
Lead with Culture by Jay Billy
Lead with Instructional Rounds by Vicki Wilson
Lead with Literacy by Mandy Ellis

Leadership & School Culture
Beyond the Surface of Restorative Practices by Marisol Rerucha
Choosing to See by Pamela Seda and Kyndall Brown
Culturize by Jimmy Casas
Escaping the School Leader's Dunk Tank by Rebecca Coda and Rick Jetter
Fight Song by Kim Bearden
From Teacher to Leader by Starr Sackstein

If the Dance Floor Is Empty, Change the Song by Joe Clark
The Innovator's Mindset by George Couros
It's OK to Say "They" by Christy Whittlesey
Kids Deserve It! by Todd Nesloney and Adam Welcome
Let Them Speak by Rebecca Coda and Rick Jetter
The Limitless School by Abe Hege and Adam Dovico
Live Your Excellence by Jimmy Casas
Next-Level Teaching by Jonathan Alsheimer
The Pepper Effect by Sean Gaillard
Principaled by Kate Barker, Kourtney Ferrua, and Rachael George
The Principled Principal by Jeffrey Zoul and Anthony McConnell
Relentless by Hamish Brewer
The Secret Solution by Todd Whitaker, Sam Miller, and Ryan Donlan
Start. Right. Now. by Todd Whitaker, Jeffrey Zoul, and Jimmy Casas
Stop. Right. Now. by Jimmy Casas and Jeffrey Zoul
Teachers Deserve It by Rae Hughart and Adam Welcome
Teach Your Class Off by CJ Reynolds
They Call Me "Mr. De" by Frank DeAngelis
Thrive through the Five by Jill M. Siler
Unmapped Potential by Julie Hasson and Missy Lennard
When Kids Lead by Todd Nesloney and Adam Dovico
Word Shift by Joy Kirr
Your School Rocks by Ryan McLane and Eric Lowe

Technology & Tools
50 Things to Go Further with Google Classroom by Alice Keeler and Libbi Miller
50 Things You Can Do with Google Classroom by Alice Keeler and Libbi Miller
140 Twitter Tips for Educators by Brad Currie, Billy Krakower, and Scott Rocco
Block Breaker by Brian Aspinall
Building Blocks for Tiny Techies by Jamila "Mia" Leonard
Code Breaker by Brian Aspinall
The Complete EdTech Coach by Katherine Goyette and Adam Juarez
Control Alt Achieve by Eric Curts
The Esports Education Playbook by Chris Aviles, Steve Isaacs, Christine Lion-Bailey, and Jesse Lubinsky

Google Apps for Littles by Christine Pinto and Alice Keeler
Master the Media by Julie Smith
Raising Digital Leaders by Jennifer Casa-Todd
Reality Bytes by Christine Lion-Bailey, Jesse Lubinsky, and
      Micah Shippee, PhD
Sail the 7 Cs with Microsoft Education by Becky Keene and
      Kathi Kersznowski
Shake Up Learning by Kasey Bell
Social LEADia by Jennifer Casa-Todd
Stepping Up to Google Classroom by Alice Keeler and Kimberly Mattina
Teaching Math with Google Apps by Alice Keeler and Diana Herrington
Teachingland by Amanda Fox and Mary Ellen Weeks
Teaching with Google Jamboard by Alice Keeler and Kimberly Mattina

Teaching Methods & Materials
All 4s and 5s by Andrew Sharos
Boredom Busters by Katie Powell
The Classroom Chef by John Stevens and Matt Vaudrey
The Collaborative Classroom by Trevor Muir
Copyrighteous by Diana Gill
CREATE by Bethany J. Petty
Ditch That Homework by Matt Miller and Alice Keeler
Ditch That Textbook by Matt Miller
Don't Ditch That Tech by Matt Miller, Nate Ridgway, and Angelia Ridgway
EDrenaline Rush by John Meehan
Educated by Design by Michael Cohen, The Tech Rabbi
The EduProtocol Field Guide by Marlena Hebern and Jon Corippo
The EduProtocol Field Guide: Book 2 by Marlena Hebern and Jon Corippo
The EduProtocol Field Guide: Math Edition by Lisa Nowakowski and
      Jeremiah Ruesch
Expedition Science by Becky Schnekser
Game On? Brain On! by Lindsay Portnoy, PhD
Guided Math AMPED by Reagan Tunstall
Innovating Play by Jessica LaBar-Twomy and Christine Pinto
Instant Relevance by Denis Sheeran
Keeping the Wonder by Jenna Copper, Ashley Bible, Abby Gross, and
      Staci Lamb
LAUNCH by John Spencer and A.J. Juliani

Make Learning MAGICAL by Tisha Richmond
Pass the Baton by Kathryn Finch and Theresa Hoover
Project-Based Learning Anywhere by Lori Elliott
Pure Genius by Don Wettrick
The Revolution by Darren Ellwein and Derek McCoy
Shift This! by Joy Kirr
Skyrocket Your Teacher Coaching by Michael Cary Sonbert
Spark Learning by Ramsey Musallam
Sparks in the Dark by Travis Crowder and Todd Nesloney
Table Talk Math by John Stevens
Unpack Your Impact by Naomi O'Brien and LaNesha Tabb
The Wild Card by Hope and Wade King
The Writing on the Classroom Wall by Steve Wyborney
You Are Poetry by Mike Johnston

Inspiration, Professional Growth & Personal Development
Be REAL by Tara Martin
Be the One for Kids by Ryan Sheehy
The Coach ADVenture by Amy Illingworth
Creatively Productive by Lisa Johnson
Educational Eye Exam by Alicia Ray
The EduNinja Mindset by Jennifer Burdis
Empower Our Girls by Lynmara Colón and Adam Welcome
Finding Lifelines by Andrew Grieve and Andrew Sharos
The Four O'Clock Faculty by Rich Czyz
How Much Water Do We Have? by Pete and Kris Nunweiler
P Is for Pirate by Dave and Shelley Burgess
A Passion for Kindness by Tamara Letter
The Path to Serendipity by Allyson Apsey
Sanctuaries by Dan Tricarico
Saving Sycamore by Molly B. Hudgens
The SECRET SAUCE by Rich Czyz
Shattering the Perfect Teacher Myth by Aaron Hogan
Stories from Webb by Todd Nesloney
Talk to Me by Kim Bearden
Teach Better by Chad Ostrowski, Tiffany Ott, Rae Hughart, and
    Jeff Gargas
Teach Me, Teacher by Jacob Chastain

Teach, Play, Learn! by Adam Peterson
The Teachers of Oz by Herbie Raad and Nathan Lang-Raad
TeamMakers by Laura Robb and Evan Robb
Through the Lens of Serendipity by Allyson Apsey
The Zen Teacher by Dan Tricarico

Children's Books
Beyond Us by Aaron Polansky
Cannonball In by Tara Martin
Dolphins in Trees by Aaron Polansky
I Want to Be a Lot by Ashley Savage
The Princes of Serendip by Allyson Apsey
Ride with Emilio by Richard Nares
The Wild Card Kids by Hope and Wade King
Zom-Be a Design Thinker by Amanda Fox

Made in the USA
Las Vegas, NV
30 October 2021